Endued With Power

How To Activate
the Gifts of the Holy Spirit
in Your Life

Endued With Power

How To Activate
the Gifts of the Holy Spirit
in Your Life

by
Norvel Hayes

HARRISON HOUSE
Tulsa, Oklahoma

Unless otherwise indicated, all Scripture quotations are taken from the *King James Version* of the Bible.

3rd Printing
Over 20,000 in Print

Endued With Power — How To Activate
the Gifts of the Holy Spirit in Your Life
ISBN 0-89274-885-0
Copyright ©1991 by Norvel Hayes
P. O. Box 1379
Cleveland, Tennessee 37311
(Formerly *Power for Living* ISBN 0-89274-707-2 and *Holy Spirit Gifts Series* ISBN 0-89274-337-9)

Published by Harrison House, Inc.
P. O. Box 35035
Tulsa, Oklahoma 74153

Contents

Endued With Power

How To Activate
the Gifts of the Holy Spirit
in Your Life

Introduction

Now concerning spiritual gifts, brethren, I would not have you ignorant...But the manifestation of the Spirit is given to every man to profit withal.

For to one is given by the Spirit the word of wisdom; to another the word of knowledge by the same Spirit;

To another faith by the same Spirit; to another the gifts of healing by the same Spirit;

To another the working of miracles; to another prophecy; to another discerning of spirits; to another divers kinds of tongues; to another the interpretation of tongues:

But all these worketh that one and the selfsame Spirit, dividing to every man severally as he will.

1 Corinthians 12:1,7-11

These nine gifts of the Spirit are very important to the Church today. They are the weapons of our warfare. A church that is trying to fight a spiritual battle without the gifts of the Spirit will never win. The Devil will rob them of the very thing God wants them to have simply because they don't know anything about the gifts of the Spirit.

The Holy Spirit is stronger than the Devil, and the gifts of the Spirit provide the power to overcome the Devil.

You might say, "Do you mean the Lord wants me to speak in tongues in a church service?" Not necessarily. The gift of tongues is a calling, a tool for public ministry. You may never do that; but He does want you to speak in tongues, to pray in the Spirit.

Praying in the Spirit, or praying in tongues, is the most powerful way to pray. God doesn't want us ignorant when it comes to praying and speaking in tongues.

You may say, "Well, my church doesn't believe in that." It doesn't make any difference what your church believes, or even what I say; it's what the Bible says that counts. The Bible is for *all* churches.

God changes not. He is not going to throw out the 12th chapter of 1 Corinthians just because you don't believe in it. It's going to operate for those who believe it. The gifts of the Spirit will operate through those who are available.

Channels For God's Power

All of us are channels for the power of God to work through. The Spirit of God rescued each of us from sin. I was in sin just like you were before the Spirit of God visited my life.

Before your spirit was reborn, you might have been a drunkard, an adulterer, a thief, or a liar. It really doesn't matter what you were or what you've done in the past. You've been forgiven. God has taken all your sins, pulled them out of you, and thrown them into the depths of a sea of forgetfulness. He has blocked them from His memory. The only ones remembering them are you and the Devil.

Don't let the Devil tell you that you're not worthy. That is a lie! God wants to use you. If you are saved, or born again, you stand before God today as white as snow — a candidate for the gifts of the Spirit.

So make your mind, your body, and your spirit available for these gifts to operate through, as the Spirit wills to use you.

How To Profit From The Gifts

But the manifestation of the Spirit is given to every man to profit withal.

1 Corinthians 12:7

The gifts of the Spirit are given to *every* man to profit him. They may be to profit you personally and not necessarily to operate through you in a public ministry.

You can profit from all of the gifts in your life personally. There will be a time in your life when you will need a miracle or a healing or more faith for a certain thing. You may need a word of prophecy. You may need to speak in tongues. You may need the interpretation of tongues.

You need to have yourself identified with a part of the Body of Christ that teaches the operation of spiritual gifts and allows them to flow freely as the Spirit wills. If the gifts are not allowed to flow in your church, then you can't reap the benefits of them. You won't profit from them. As long as you live, you will be robbed.

Make Yourself Available

If the people of the Church would be willing to let the gifts of the Spirit operate through them, the gifts would be manifested more. But some church people are afraid to move out in the gifts in public because they don't know what to expect.

You may think, ''God would never use me like that. I'm not worthy.'' Make yourself available and see if He will use you. *He will!* He will use you as the Spirit wills.

The eyes of the Lord are searching back and forth across the land — up and down the pews of every church in America — looking for individuals who are willing to be used by Him. Before the Holy Ghost can manifest Himself, He must have vessels to operate through.

1

From Heaven Come God's Weapons For the Church

From the Spirit flows victory for everybody that belongs to God's Church; for everybody that believes in the power of the Spirit.

> **Now there are diversities of gifts, but the same Spirit. And there are differences of administrations, but the same Lord. And there are diversities of operations, but it is the same God which worketh all in all. But the manifestation of the Spirit is given to every man to profit withal.**
>
> **1 Corinthians 12:4-7**

You might say, "Well, I got a manifestation from the Spirit, I got blessed."

Brother and Sister, Jesus blesses you because He loves you. Jesus could bless you today, but you could die next week with cancer. Is that clear? You get things from God because you *believe the Bible.*

There is a lot more in the Bible to believe than just believing that God is a good God. Now God is a good God and you're supposed to believe that God is a good God. But God has things He wants to *give* you.

He's got nine gifts He has given to the Church. And all those manifestations are supposed to be manifested in the Church. They are given to profit withal — to every man and to every woman, to everybody that belongs to God's

Church. They come down from heaven. *They are called weapons.*

> **For the weapons of our warfare are not carnal, but mighty through God to the pulling down of strong holds.**
>
> **2 Corinthians 10:4**

You're in a battle. You say, ''What do you mean I'm in a battle? The battle has already been won. It's already been won by Jesus.''

But you're not Jesus. Is that clear?

The battle has already been won by Jesus. The price has already been paid. On the cross, the price has already been paid by the stripes on His back for your healing. He's already been to hell. He's already taken the keys away from the devil.

He's got a set of keys to give you.

Jesus said, *The Church that I build, the gates of hell shall not prevail against it.* But the Church needs the gifts of the Spirit operating in it, God's weapons, to let you in on what the Devil is trying to do to you.

The gifts give you power, by faith, to do anything. Bring healing, miracles. Tongues and interpretation build you up. Prophecy to build the whole church up.

Jesus said, *When you get born again by the Spirit of God and become part of the Church, I'll give to you a set of keys, Believer.*

And that's all you are ever going to get. That's all, on this earth. You inherited heaven when you got born again. But this is the thing that the Lord Jesus Christ wants you to understand: you're not in heaven, yet. You're living here. You have to work every day. And you have to fight devils.

Jesus said, **I will give unto thee the keys of the kingdom of heaven...** (Matt. 16:19). There are a lot of things in the kingdom of heaven. But that's no sign that you'll ever get them. It all depends if you find the right key or not.

There is one key on the great key ring of God that says divine healing. That's no sign that you'll ever be healed, though. It all depends on if you take the time to dig into God's word and find the key to healing. Even after you find it, you have to pull it out of there and take it and stick it into heaven by faith. And you have to turn it yourself (put action to your faith). And when you do it, healing flows down to you.

I had a good Christian mother who died with cancer at 37 years of age leaving three little children on the earth crying and wringing their hands because their mother was gone, never to come home again. I was a ten-year-old cotton-headed boy when my mother died. She never found the key to healing.

After I prayed and went into heaven and God started talking to me, I said, "Why didn't my mother get healed, Jesus? She loved you."

He said, "The church she went to never taught her anything about how to receive my divine healing power."

You only know what you've been taught.

There is a key on God's key ring that says success, financial success. Most people never find it.

There is a key on there that says spiritual success: God takes you into the things of the Spirit.

God wants the things of the Spirit to go forth. There are all kinds of good things in the set of keys that Jesus gives to the believer. But if you're not a student of the Scriptures, you'll never find the key. That's the sad and sick part. If you don't study the Scriptures, and don't take time to dig and read, you won't ever get it.

Things from heaven, all things in the New Testament, fall on you because you believe the Bible and *your faith pulls them out of heaven down to earth to you.*

Jesus said, **The Church that I build, the gates of hell shall not prevail against it.** It's not fair for sick people to walk into the church and have to go home sick. Have the ministry of the laying on of hands and I'll guarantee you, God's healing power will flow from your hands into the sick person.

Go out to the byways, to your neighbors and lay hands on them in Jesus' name and watch the healing power of God go into them. Some of them will accept it and some won't; but that won't have anything to do with it. It will come through you.

Jesus has given you the keys. Read the Bible for yourself and find out what's in there. Memorize what you get from God. Know and memorize the twelfth chapter of First Corinthians. If you'll get that chapter in you, it'll be just like anything else — when you need something, the Holy Spirit will come and begin to manifest Himself to help you. I don't care if it's the gift of faith, the gift of the working of miracles, or what it is. But He'll come as the Spirit wills. You can't make God do it.

> For to one is given by the Spirit the word of wisdom; to another the word of knowledge by the same Spirit; To another faith by the same Spirit; to another the gifts of healings by the same Spirit; To another the working of miracles; to another prophecy; to another discerning of spirits; to another divers kinds of tongues; to another the interpretation of tongues; But all these worketh that one and the selfsame Spirit, dividing to every man severally as he will.
>
> For as the body is one, and hath many members, and all the members of that one body, being many are one body: so also is Christ...But now hath God set the members every one of them in the body, as it hath pleased him. And if they were all one member, where were the body? But now are they many members, yet but one body. And the eye cannot say unto the hand, I have no need of thee: nor again the head to the feet, I have no need of you.
>
> 1 Corinthians 12:8-12,18-21

You need all the gifts of the Spirit. You can't say, ''I've got healing. I don't need miracles.'' Or, ''I've got miracles,

I don't need prophecy." Or, "I've got wisdom, I don't need tongues and interpretation."

God says you're going to need every one of them. There's coming a time in your life when you'll need every one of the gifts of the Spirit, because they are God's weapons to fight the devil with.

The *gift of faith* is a gift of power where God's power explodes and comes on you and changes you into what God needs you to be at that moment. The *gift of healing* is God's healing power that comes into manifestation all of a sudden. The third power gift is the *working of miracles*.

There are three revelation gifts. The *word of wisdom* points toward the future. The *word of knowledge* is a manifestation of the Spirit where God shows you the condition of things in your house, in your business, in somebody's life that He wants you to help. The other revelation gift is the *discerning of spirits*. The Holy Spirit will manifest Himself and show you some spirit that He doesn't want you involved in, a spirit that's not of God.

The vocal gifts are prophecy, tongues, and interpretation. Prophecy is when God's power comes to you and the Holy Spirit manifests Himself on the inside of you and the ministry gift begins to boil up supernaturally, words in a known language (words that you know) that God wants you to get up and speak out. *Tongues:* the Spirit of God will manifest Himself and tongues will begin to flow out of you. Then God's power will come on another person in manifestation and give him the *interpretation* to explain and tell in English what you said in tongues.

That's God power. That's the sum and substance of the gifts of the Spirit.

Getting into Shape to Receive

"How can I get myself in shape to receive the gifts of the Spirit?" you ask.

There is only one way that I know of. *You first of all have to be delivered from yourself.*

How do you do that?

By the *fire of God.*

Remember on the day of Pentecost when God sent fire with His Spirit? *The fire of God follows God's Spirit.*

What does fire do? It burns. The fire of God burns, demolishes, does away, makes things disappear that don't need to be there.

There are so many full gospel people that should know better but don't know very much about the fire of God. The fire of God is so important to get a person delivered, to burn the chaff out.

In other words, you have to be delivered from yourself so you can receive what the Holy Ghost wants to give you. Whether you know it or not, *you are your own worst enemy.*

You can't go by what somebody else does. You have to pray, get hold of God, and worship God yourself.

Your mate may worship God three hours a day and pray two hours a day, but that's not going to get you any victory from heaven. You've got to do it yourself. Jesus is a personal Jesus. You can't live on your mate's experience from God. You can't live on your relatives' experience from God.

You can't live with God because your mother was a good Christian. You've got to bow down your knees before Almighty God yourself and make Him the living God of your life.

The Spirit world is real. *And all of these beautiful gifts that God wants to give to you are weapons from God to the Church.* They are weapons to do away with the works of the devil. God doesn't want His believers, His children, putting up with the Devil.

And you wouldn't have to put up with him if you didn't listen to him. Jesus said, *Don't listen to the Devil. You can't believe anything he says. The truth is not in him.*

You just have to watch his deceiving power. He'll try to put a part of a truth over to you. And, oh, it will seem so right to you. But after you've done it, you'll say, "How did I ever get into this mess?"

You didn't pray through and get the mind of God. You did it just because it *seemed* right.

The Devil will give you four or five things that seem right and tell you one big lie so he can trick you and get you all goofed up, messed up, weak and confused.

But God's got weapons to let you know what's going on.

Be willing to listen to the three vocal gifts: tongues, interpretations, prophecy. When they roll out of somebody supernaturally, and the Holy Spirit witnesses to you, be willing to study the interpretation, study prophecy.

Now, why can't you receive those weapons from God?

Is there some reason why you can't receive those nine gifts of the Spirit like you're supposed to? Sure there is.

> For what the law could not do, in that it was weak through the flesh, God sending his own Son in the likeness of sinful flesh, and for sin, condemned sin in the flesh: That the righteousness of the law might be fulfilled in us, who walk not after the flesh, but after the Spirit.
>
> **Romans 8:3,4**

You see, the righteousness of the law is not going to be fulfilled in you unless you walk after the Spirit. *You have to be hungry for the Spirit.*

> For they that are after the flesh do mind the things of the flesh; but they that are after the Spirit the things of the Spirit. For to be carnally minded is death; but to be spiritually minded is life and peace.
>
> For if ye live after the flesh, ye shall die: but if ye through the Spirit do mortify the deeds of the body, ye shall

live. For as many as are led by the Spirit of God, they are the sons of God.

Romans 8:5,6,13,14

The sons and daughters of God are robbed for only one reason — not two — just one: Because they are not led by the Spirit of God.

For ye have not received the spirit of bondage again to fear; but ye have received the Spirit of adoption, whereby we cry, Abba, Father.

Romans 8:15

The Spirit of adoption where we cry Father. We walk around crying *Father.*

"Oh, Father, healing is for me. Oh, Father, mercies are for me. Father, the gifts of the Spirit are for me. Father, a clear mind is for me. Father, financial success is for me."

But you have to *say that it's for you.* As long as you *wonder,* it won't work. God doesn't answer wondering prayers. He answers faith prayers. He answers confession prayers.

The Spirit itself beareth witness with our spirit, that we are the children of God.

Romans 8:16

Does the Spirit of God ever manifest Himself to you? That's a sign that you're a child of God.

If you and I are children of God, why don't we believe our Father? If we'd only believe Him, we could receive everything He wants to give us.

He is the Father and you are the child. And the Spirit that is in you will bear witness that you are a child of God.

The Bible says that your Father will not withhold one good thing from you.

It Isn't Easy

You might say, "Is it easy to yield yourself to the Spirit of God?"

16

No, it's not.

And when it first starts in your life, it will usually scare you. It did me.

The Lord Jesus tried to get me to prophesy. He put words in me and tried to get me to prophesy, and I'd hold on to the church pew. He'd shake me and I'd cry. I would weep and hold on to the church pew. I would not do it. It scared me too bad.

He would boil up in me, giving me the words, but I didn't want to get up and say them out. I loved the Lord. But *I was afraid I'd say something wrong.* And I just wouldn't do it. I mean, for two or three years I hung on to the back of the pew.

Oh, tongues and interpretation can bring confidence to you. It can build a foundation in you.

I was in Tulsa, Oklahoma, at Brother Hagin's apartment late one Sunday afternoon. We were having a little prayer meeting. Brother and Sister Goodwin were also there.

All of a sudden Sister Goodwin came over to me and started speaking in tongues. And when she got through, Brother Goodwin just walked over, and this is the word that he said to me. "Now Son, those words that I've been putting in you, I want you to get up and speak those words out. Now I want you to go home and I want you to get permission from your pastor to get up in the church and speak those words out. If your pastor refuses you, I'm going to give you the ministry anyway (but just not there, in other words)."

I went home and asked the pastor. I said, "Jesus said for me to come and get permission from you. When the Lord puts prophecy on me, words on me, do you want to give me permission to speak them out?"

"Oh yes, Brother Norvel," he said. "You know you can obey God in this church. Just go ahead and obey the Lord."

So I said, "Well, we'll just have to wait and see."

And sure enough, it came about two weeks later on Sunday night, at the end of the service. God moved on me, and melted me.

Since that tongues and interpretation, I'd been thinking about that. And that ministered to me, gave me strength and confidence.

I got up and spoke them out. After I spoke them out, as soon as I got the last word out, God came on me so strong and started blessing me so much, I just fell on my knees and started crying and weeping and getting blessed.

I found out God loves me and He was petting me because I obeyed the Holy Spirit.

When God was training me and bringing me up in those days and trying to mold me, oh He'd bless me.

I'd start reading the Bible in the morning in bed. I'd get so involved and scriptures would start jumping out at me. The Lord would begin to shake me and I couldn't read the Bible anymore. I'd just lie down there, tears coming up out of my eyes, just streaming down my cheeks. I felt like all my bones were going to jump out.

Sometimes He would shake me from 8 o'clock until noon. My bed would shake for three or four hours. I mean my bed would shake. I couldn't even stop. I would just be saying, "Oh, Jesus, Jesus." Talk about getting blessed!

So the gifts began to operate through me, because I was ministered to by a precious couple that the Holy Ghost operated through that knew how to minister to me. The Spirit of God knew exactly what I wanted and what I needed. I needed Brother and Sister Goodwin to minister to me. I needed for God to tell me, "I'm putting words in you, and son, I want you to get up and speak them out."

Tongues and Interpretation
— A Mighty Weapon

It is important that you listen to what the Spirit of God says to you. You have to have the right message, the right time.

I was in Jackson, Mississippi, at a Full Gospel Convention. I was one of the speakers.

Dr. Keller (who was in charge) came up to me and said, "Norvel, I don't know the reason, but the Spirit of God said to get you to speak tonight about 15 to 20 minutes before I put on the main speaker."

Ken Copeland was one of the speakers at the convention, but he was not speaking that night; but he was sitting on the platform with a number of other people.

I got up and began to speak. I was giving a testimony about doing some street work, working with dope addicts. I was telling how I got an alcoholic saved in front of a Dairy Queen.

I had been speaking about 17 minutes, when all of a sudden, tongues came forth in the congregation — powerful. Ken Copeland gave the interpretation. It lasted about 22 minutes.

In that interpretation that Ken spoke out, he told me the reason God had found favor in me was because of my bold, uncompromising position upon His Word. God said, "Son, I'm going to take you in three different manifestations. I'm going to take you into the spirit world. I'm going to show you and unfold to you the entire operation of the Devil's kingdom, and how he operates."

And He already has. He's taken me through the air, three different manifestations, and let me float through the air. Float over the cities. Float down the streets. Float just like a chicken hawk. He let me float through the air backwards and forward, just like demons, lurking, hungry, seeking desperately, trying to find some human being that they can live in. They are looking for a house of flesh, that's made in the image of God.

Their master hates God so much. They want to get in the flesh that is made in the image of God. If they go too long and can't find somebody to get into, they will live in animals, for a while. But if they can, they want to get inside of a human being.

They don't get in a hurry. Demons just go backward and forward like a bunch of chicken hawks in slow motion. There are not just a few thousand of them either, there are hundreds of thousands of them in the air that don't have bodies to live in. And they want bodies to live in.

They are going to try to get your body, *try*. They can't ever live in your body as long as you belong to God's Church and you bow down to God and worship Him. Not as long as you live your life for God. Not as long as you pray and read your Bible. Demons will never live in your body, never.

You see, *demons are personalities without a body.* When a particular demon gets inside of a person, that person becomes what that demon is. The longer the demon operates through that person, the stronger he gets and the more wicked the person gets.

One manifestation of tongues and interpretation can blast that person into the kingdom of God and make him repent.

One prophecy can come from a man's lips and so blast that person, if they're sitting there, that they'll fall on the floor and repent before God.

That's how important the weapons of God's warfare are.

Ministry of Intercession

Praying in tongues can also be used in a ministry of intercession for someone else.

My pastor in Cleveland, Tennessee, came by my office one day. He had built several new rooms onto the church and needed some carpeting. He said, "I'm going to the rug manufacturer, and God said He wants you to go with me."

When we met with the owner of the rug company, he walked us through his plant. As they were talking together and looking at several rolls of carpeting, the word of the Lord came to me so sweetly, saying, "Walk over to the right and pray in the Spirit."

Praying in the Spirit means praying in tongues. The Apostle Paul said, **I will pray with the spirit, and I will pray with the understanding also** (1 Cor. 14:15). There are two different ways to pray — in your own language and in the Spirit (in tongues).

So I walked over to my right and began to pray in tongues. The Spirit of prayer was on me very gently. For about five minutes I walked back and forth, praying quietly in the Spirit. Then it just lifted from me.

When I walked back to where my pastor was standing, he said, "Norvel, while you were gone, this man decided to give me all these rugs for the church. We can have it all free!"

That supernatural deal came about through the prayer of intercession, praying in tongues.

Intercession is a ministry.

If you are called to intercession, you may wake up at three o'clock some morning and begin to pray and cry and groan in the Spirit. Then all of a sudden, you may start laughing. At times you may feel pain in your body, sometimes so severe that all you can do is groan in the Spirit.

21

Intercession can be hard work at times. Sometimes God lets you feel the pain of another person as you are in intercession for him. You may have to live the life of a heart attack patient for a while. You may feel pain in your legs like a crippled man suffers.

It is important that you know what is taking place during those times. You must know God, know the moving of His Spirit, and realize the obligation you have to the Holy Ghost.

If God has called you to the ministry of intercession, you need to know what He wants you to do. If you are standing in intercession for someone who is suffering a heart attack, your intercession could save him.

Most of the time you won't even know who you are interceding for, but sometimes the Lord will show you who it is.

If you are called as an intercessor, sometimes you will have to pray for hours and hours and hours. Sometimes God will obligate you to pray all night long!

One day while I was in my office working, God moved on me to intercede for someone, so I had to keep everybody out of my office. God showed me that I was interceding for a boy and girl who were about to separate. There was conflict in their marriage and she was about to have a baby.

When the Spirit of intercession came upon me, I just fell over on the couch in my office and began to intercede for them. I thought I was through, so I walked out into the hall; but while I was talking to some people, it came on me again. I had to get a chair and sit down to keep from falling on the floor. Then the Holy Ghost let me know that I wasn't through interceding for them, that I hadn't stayed in God's presence long enough to get the complete victory in it.

Knowing What To Pray

I don't always know what or how to pray, and neither will you. God didn't make us that smart!

It says in the Word of God that the Spirit makes intercession for us because we don't know how we should pray:

> **Likewise the Spirit also helpeth our infirmities: for we know not what we should pray for as we ought: but the Spirit itself maketh intercession for us with groanings which cannot be uttered.**
>
> **And he that searcheth the hearts knoweth what is the mind of the Spirit, because he maketh intercession for the saints according to the will of God.**
>
> **Romans 8:26,27**

What is the will of God? The Bible — God's Word. The Bible says that God sent the Lord Jesus to heal you, so don't ever think, "I wonder if it's God's will to heal that man or that woman." Just know it is His will to heal them because Jesus said that what He did for one, He would do for the other. He sent His Word to heal *all*!

Peace, contentment, victory, and health have been sent from heaven to you — thanks to the Lord Jesus Christ!

Getting Things Through Intercession

You can get things through intercession if God can trust you with them.

Lester Sumrall is one man who believes in praying more than anybody I have ever seen in my life. While I was holding a meeting in his church one time, he said, "Norvel, come with me. I want to take you for a ride."

We got into his car and drove out to a television station. Brother Sumrall said, "See that station right there? That thing shows a bunch of junk all the time; but I want that television station for God, and I believe He wants me to have it. I got you out here to pray and ask God to give it to me. You pray and I'll agree with you."

So I started praying. I pointed at that television station and claimed it for God, in Jesus' name. In two years, Brother Sumrall owned that station — debt free!

When you go to prayer like that, your inward man has to be strong enough to know what you want from God and what God wants you to have.

You are not going to be able to do that unless you have power in the inward man.

Power To Save Lives

If I had not known about the power of the Holy Spirit for the inward man, if I had not been willing to be led by the Holy Spirit of God, if I had not known the power of praying in the Spirit, there is a good chance that my daughter would be dead today.

One night in my spirit, I saw my daughter Zona dead. I had no earthly idea that anything was wrong with her, but in the Spirit I knew there was something very, very wrong. I went to her home, got her husband off to the side, and said, "Bob, there is something wrong with Zona, but I can't put my finger on it. Do you know of anything that's wrong with her?"

He said, "No, not for sure."

All night while I stayed in their home, I could feel in my spirit that there was something seriously wrong. I said, "Zona, honey, is there something wrong? Have you got something you want to tell me?"

She said, "No." She didn't even know there was anything wrong.

The only thing I could do was pray in the Spirit. I didn't know what to pray for, but I had seen her dead and I knew I had to pray. She is the only child I have, and I didn't want her to die; so I interceded for her that night.

Within a few days after I prayed for her, something happened at the bank where she worked and she had to go to the doctor for an examination. When she went in, he found out that she didn't have much potassium in her body.

"Zona," he said, "you have the least amount of potassium in your body of anyone I have ever examined. What in the world has happened to you? You should be dead. Did you know that? You have a strong heart, but you are ready to collapse any day."

The doctor admitted her to the hospital and pumped potassium into her bloodstream. He told her, "It's going to take several days to get your body functioning normally again. You should have collapsed days ago."

I know the reason she didn't collapse: I was praying. Intercessory prayer kept her alive until she could see the doctor and get the help she needed.

Pleasing God

God manifested Himself through the Spirit on Zona's behalf, but you have to please God to do that. You can't please God as long as you say you don't believe in the gifts of the Spirit. If you don't put emphasis on the power of the gifts of the Spirit, you will be blinded by the power of the Devil and he will run over you. You won't get the blessings of God to flow in your church or your own personal life.

The supernatural blessings can only flow in a place where the Word is presented and where you please God.

If you are ashamed of God's healing power, God won't heal people in your church. If you refuse to have a healing service in your church, God won't heal people there; and He won't heal your family either as long as you refuse Him and His gifts.

So many times when people die, we say, "Well, it was the Lord's will." No! No! No! It wasn't the Lord's will; the Bible is the Lord's will!

I didn't know what to pray for my daughter, but I did know God's will in the matter. I prayed in the Spirit because my inward man was strong enough to pray, and the Holy Ghost was able to work. He worked it out so that Zona could be examined by the doctor. The Holy Ghost did that — not me. The Devil was planning to kill her. Had it not been for the Holy Ghost, she would have collapsed. If my spirit man had not been built up to the point that I could pray and keep her before God, she probably would have died.

The Devil comes to kill people who have weak spirits. You can have a strong body; but if you have a weak spirit, the Devil can kill you.

But be encouraged! The Spirit of God is bigger and stronger than the Devil! If you will obey the Holy Ghost, the Spirit of the Living God, He will do mighty things for you.

God doesn't answer prayers for weak people. Why? Because if they are weak, they don't believe it themselves.

You have to show God what you believe, and you have to show the Devil, too.

Developing Power In Your Inward Man

If you will build up the inward man, you will be able to rise up with authority, speak to the Devil in Jesus' name, and command him to go — and he will have to leave!

God moves by His Spirit, and He will show you many things if you will keep your spirit built up. You must have power in your inward man in order for God to work in your behalf.

How do you get it? You read the Bible and feed your spirit good food every day. Then you obey the Bible — you do what God says.

With power built up in your inward man, you can come against destruction. You can make intercession in Jesus' name, and God's power will change things for you. He will change things, not part of the time, but all the time!

> **But ye, beloved, building up yourselves on your most holy faith, praying in the Holy Ghost,**
>
> **Keep yourselves in the love of God, looking for the mercy of our Lord Jesus Christ unto eternal life.**
>
> **Jude 20,21**

2

The Word of Wisdom

First Corinthians 12:1 states:

Now concerning spiritual gifts, brethren, I would not have you ignorant.

Remember, this gift is no different from the "gifts of healing," or any of the rest of the gifts of the Spirit. God does not want you ignorant concerning the *word of wisdom*. As you learn the meaning of *the gift of the word of wisdom*, and how badly you need it, you will find how exciting that it can be in your own life.

Paul says in verse 8: **For to one is given by the Spirit the word of wisdom....** What does he mean?

The *gift of the word of wisdom* is a word of God's knowledge of what is going to take place in the future, a divine revelation of future events.

You may say, "Why do I need *the gift of the word of wisdom?*"

To answer that, let's read 1 Corinthians 12 again and see what Paul has to say about the spiritual gifts:

Now concerning spiritual gifts, brethren, I would not have you ignorant. Ye know that ye were Gentiles, carried away unto these dumb idols, even as ye were led.

Wherefore I give you to understand, that no man speaking by the Spirit of God calleth Jesus accursed: and that no man can say that Jesus is the Lord, but by the Holy Ghost.

> Now there are diversities of gifts, but the same Spirit. And there are differences of administrations, but the same Lord. And there are diversities of operations, but it is the same God which worketh all in all.
>
> But the manifestation of the Spirit is given to every man to profit withal.
>
> **1 Corinthians 12:1-7**

Each *gift of the Spirit* has its place. One cannot take the place of the other. Each gift has its own distinct way of helping you during your life, and each gift is given by the Holy Ghost. As we just read, "the manifestation of the Spirit is given to every man to profit withal."

The *word of wisdom* is given to you for your own private life. It is given to you to help you.

> For to one is given by the Spirit the word of wisdom...
>
> **verse 8**

Many times, *the word of wisdom* will operate through a person to an individual or to a group of people in public assembly. Most Christians never have that operating in their life unless they are called into the public ministry. But all Christians can have the *word of wisdom* operating in their lives for themselves. They can have that same gift to operate in their own personal lives, and also to help their friends. It works the same way. Look again at First Corinthians 12:8-12,18

> For to one is given by the Spirit the word of wisdom; to another the word of knowledge by the same Spirit; To another faith by the same Spirit; to another the gifts of healing by the same Spirit;
>
> To another the working of miracles; to another prophecy; to another discerning of spirits; to another divers kinds of tongues; to another the interpretation of tongues:
>
> But all these worketh that one and the selfsame Spirit, dividing to every man severally as he will. For as the body is one, and hath many members, and all the members of that one body, being many, are one body: so also is Christ.
>
> But now hath God set the members every one of them in the body, as it has pleased him.

You see, we are supposed to be so close together, just as the parts of the human body are joined together. When we are born again we become members of the Body of Christ. We are brothers and sisters in Christ, and we are supposed to be absolutely in love with each other. God has set the members in the Body of Christ exactly where He wants them.

> **And if they were all one member, where were the body? But now are they many members, yet but one body. And the eye cannot say unto the hand, I have no need of thee: nor again the head to the feet, I have no need of you.**
>
> **verses 19-21**

You can't look over to the person next to you and say, "I have no need of you. I have been making it all these years without you. I don't even know you, and I don't need you." You need them! You need their love.

Ten years from now, they may move next door to you. And sometime when you are in trouble, the Holy Ghost may give them *a word of wisdom* for you; to tell you something that is going to happen to you in the future. They can walk over to your house and knock on your door and say, "Oh! I've got to talk to you! The Lord told me something that is going to happen to you. He showed me in a vision."

That is how God gets His knowledge over to the human race. He is the supernatural God, the spiritual God; we are natural people. He gives *His word of wisdom* to us through the power of the Holy Ghost within us.

You need the spiritual *gift of the word of wisdom* working in your life.

Wisdom In Old Testament Men

Back in Old Testament times, most all of the old prophets had *the word of wisdom* operating in their lives, to show them what was going to happen in the future. In fact, the prophet Elisha told the children of Israel all about their enemies. He told them what their enemies were going to do, and what they could do about it. (See 2 Kings 6:8-12.)

God gave a *word of wisdom* to Noah when He manifested Himself to Noah in Genesis 6. He told Noah that it was going to rain, and then explained in detail how to build an ark.

It didn't rain for over a hundred years, but God told Noah that something was going to happen in the future. Notice, beginning with verse 11:

> The earth also was corrupt before God, and the earth was filled with violence. And God looked upon the earth, and, behold, it was corrupt; for all flesh had corrupted his way upon the earth.
>
> And God said unto Noah, The end of all flesh is come before me; for the earth is filled with violence through them; and, behold, I will destroy them with the earth.
>
> 2 Kings 6:11-13

God then said in verses 14 and 15: **Make thee an ark of gopher wood; rooms shalt thou make in the ark, and shalt pitch it within and without with pitch. And this is the fashion which thou shalt make it of....** God went on to tell Noah what to put on the ark. Noah received that *word of wisdom* from God and eight people were saved to replenish the earth, as well as every species of animal — **all that in whose nostrils was the breath of life.**

Paul and a Word of God's Wisdom

A prime example in the New Testament of someone who availed himself of the *gift of the word of wisdom* was Paul. Paul received *a word of God's wisdom* when it looked as though there was no hope. More than forty men had said, "I am going to eat nothing and drink nothing until Paul dies!" That is pretty strong. It is bad enough to have two or three men after you to kill you, but when all the leaders say that you are going to die, and forty men say that they aren't going to eat or drink until you are dead, that is serious.

From the natural, how in the world could Paul know what was God's will? Paul was a human being, just like you and me. He didn't know everything in the natural. But Paul had the Holy Ghost living within him. The only thing that Paul knew more than you is what the Holy Ghost gave him through *the word of wisdom.* Paul wrote over half of the New Testament because the Holy Ghost came upon him. The Holy Ghost wrote the New Testament through Paul and others. He gave to them great *words of wisdom.*

We read in Acts 23:11: **And the night following the Lord stood by him, and said, Be of good cheer, Paul: for as thou hast testified of me in Jerusalem, so must thou bear witness also at Rome.** That is all Paul needed!

Paul said (in other words), "I am not going to die. It doesn't make any difference how many people are fasting for my death or how many leaders say that they are going to kill me. I don't care how many jails I am in, or how much blood is running off me, or how badly they beat me! I am going to preach at Rome because God said that I am to be of good cheer. As I have testified of Him in Jerusalem, so must I bear witness in Rome!"

If you read the life of Paul, you will find that he always wanted to go to Rome and preach. So he said, "Before I die and leave this earth, I am going to preach at Rome. God said so, and that is the way it is!"

The gift of the word of wisdom worked through Paul.

Word of Wisdom Through An Angel

God can use you to give yourself *a word of wisdom* through the Holy Ghost that is within you. He can use another person to give you *the word of wisdom,* and He can use angels. Such was the case with Cornelius. God sent an

33

angel to Cornelius' house to tell him what to do, and who to talk to, and what would happen to him if he would obey God. Though Cornelius wasn't saved, he was praying, and God heard Cornelius' prayer.

Many people pray, yet they are not saved. They believe that Jesus is real. They have great respect for God. But nobody has ever taken the time to tell them how to get saved. They only have a vague intellectual vision of God and Jesus. They have a great respect for Him, but have never been born again.

Cornelius was that type of person. He had a good heart about him, but he was not born again. You can read about Cornelius' experience in Acts 10. I will paraphrase it.

Cornelius had been praying up to the throne of God, and the Holy Ghost showed Cornelius what to do. An angel appeared to him and said, ''Send some men down to Joppa. There is a man down there by the name of Peter, living in a certain house. Ask Peter to come up here. He will give you the words whereby you and your household shall be saved.'' That was a point of *God's knowledge through a word of wisdom from God* as to what was going to happen in the future. Cornelius had a part to play, just as many times an individual has a part to play if something is to come to pass or not.

The angel could not tell Cornelius how to get saved, but he, through the Holy Ghost using him, could tell Cornelius who to go to for the information on how to get saved. Cornelius did as the angel told him; he sent men down to Joppa, and they brought Peter back with them, because the Spirit of God had been working on Peter also. Peter obeyed the Spirit of God, and as a result, Cornelius and his entire household was saved when the Holy Ghost fell on them.

You Need God's Word of Wisdom

It is when God gives you *the word of His wisdom* to use: to let you know what is going on, or what is to take place in the future, that you can talk about being successful in your undertakings. Through *the word of God's wisdom* you can find out exactly what you need in your daily life, and exactly the way the situation is.

The second chapter of First Corinthians concerns the revelation of God to man:

> And I, brethren, when I came to you, came not with excellency of speech or wisdom, declaring unto you the testimony of God.
>
> For I determined not to know any thing among you, save Jesus Christ, and him crucified.
>
> And I was with you in weakness, and in fear, and in much trembling.
>
> And my speech and my preaching was not with enticing words of man's wisdom, but in demonstration of the Spirit and of power:
>
> That your faith should not stand in the wisdom of men, but in the power of God.
>
> Howbeit we speak wisdom among them that are perfect: yet not the wisdom of this world, nor of the princes of this world, that come to nought:
>
> But we speak the wisdom of God in a mystery, even the hidden wisdom, which God ordained before the world unto our glory.
>
> 1 Corinthians 2:1-7

Let me emphasize verse 7: **But we speak the wisdom of God in a mystery, even the hidden wisdom, which God ordained before the world unto our glory.** Please study that verse! You can get a glimpse of God's love for you in there. God wants to give you His mind.

> Which none of the princes of this world knew: for had they known it, they would not have crucified the Lord of glory. But as it is written, Eye hath not seen, nor ear heard,

35

neither have entered into the heart of man, the things which
God hath prepared for them that love him.

But God hath revealed them unto us by his Spirit: for
the Spirit searcheth all things, yea, the deep things of God.
For what man knoweth the things of a man, save the spirit
of man which is in him? even so the things of God knoweth
no man, but the Spirit of God.

1 Corinthians 2:8-11

You can't get God's ideas on things unless the Holy
Ghost gives them to you. The Holy Ghost knows the mind
of God: you don't. If you want to know the real truth about
anything, you have to get it from the Spirit of God Who
lives inside you.

Have you ever heard anybody say, "Well, I thought
that it was the Lord's will. But it must not have been. This
is a mess! I'm not sure it is the Lord's will for me to get
married."

Well, if things are a mess, it was not the Lord's will!
It was your will. You decided that. The Holy Ghost did not
tell you to do it. In fact, that is the problem with most
American homes today. God didn't put most husbands and
wives together. They put themselves together.

Now we have received, not the spirit of the world, but
the spirit which is of God; that we might know the things
that are freely given to us of God.

1 Corinthians 2:12

We need to know that the things freely given to us come
from the Lord. And we do this by allowing our spirit man
to listen to the Spirit of God, as He gives us *the word of
wisdom:* to know what is to come in our lives.

Which things also we speak, not in words which man's
wisdom teacheth, but which the Holy Ghost teacheth;
comparing spiritual things with spiritual.

1 Corinthians 2:13

That is where people get mixed up. We should not
listen to what man's wisdom tells us: we should listen to
what the Holy Ghost Who lives down in our belly teaches.

> But the natural man receiveth not the things of the Spirit
> of God: for they are foolishness unto him: neither can he
> know them, because they are spiritually discerned.
>
> 1 Corinthians 2:14

If you would ask a person if the Holy Ghost is in his belly, he would think that was foolishness. The natural man cannot receive the things of the Spirit of God. He cannot discern them, because they are not naturally discerned.

You can't have *the word of wisdom* working for you unless you are born again. *You need to be born again, and baptized with the Holy Ghost.* People who live in sin obey the Devil. They do not operate *the gifts of the Spirit.*

> But he that is spiritual judgeth all things, yet he himself
> is judged of no man. For who hath known the mind of the
> Lord, that he may instruct him? But we have the mind of
> Christ.
>
> 1 Corinthians 2:15,16

If you have the mind of the Lord, you are not going to make mistakes. I can look back on my past and there were a lot of things in which I did not have the mind of Christ. I just did it on my own, just as you. You did it from the natural standpoint; just because you wanted to do it.

We just read that the natural man doesn't understand the things of God. You cannot understand God's will for you in life, as long as you are in the natural. Unless you pray and read the Bible, you cannot know the will of God. You may belong to a church, but if you never read the Bible, and never pray, and somebody came and knocked on your door, and said, ''God told me to tell you this:...'' you would not accept it. Why?

Because you would think that it was foolishness. Get in the Word of God. Pray. Then if somebody comes to give you *a word of wisdom* about what is to come to pass in your life, you can accept it. You will understand that the Holy Ghost is telling you something, through that person, that is going to happen to you in the future.

This gift is very important in your life. *A word of God's wisdom,* imparted unto you (the knowledge of God), will save you from making a bunch of *dumb mistakes* and falling into *valleys and ditches.* It is very important for you to allow this gift to operate through you. Claim it.

A lot of Christians do not understand this, and they will say, "Well, Brother Norvel, how do I get these gifts?"

Claim them. Just as you do when you claim a healing. Say, "Thank You, Jesus. The 12th chapter of 1 Corinthians is mine. Thank You, Lord, for *the word of wisdom.* It is mine. Thank You, Lord, for *the gifts of healing.* It is mine." He will give you a *word of wisdom,* today: *now.*

God Gave Me a Vision

A few years ago, there was a meeting at Howard University in Washington, D.C. The Lord said for me to go to that meeting. I packed my clothes, caught a plane, and went to the Washington, D.C. airport. I had no idea that I was going to get *a word of God's wisdom* about what is going to come upon the earth in the future.

Howard University is where they were having the riots, back in the "Berkeley days." That was when the kids would pile up hundreds of chairs in front of the gates, and do all kinds of dumb things. They were having riots on just about every campus across the country. But I went in there and said, "Here I am. The Lord sent me in here."

I met the University chaplain, and he said, "I've got three different places where you can stay." He started naming them off. One was the home of a Catholic priest.

I said, "Well, I might as well stay with a priest!" They took me down to the house and there were about six Catholic priests in the place. I met them all, and they took me upstairs to the bedroom. I was there at the wishes of the conference. They were cooperating with the conference.

A Word of Wisdom From God

When the priests left, I knelt down beside my bed to pray. All of a sudden, while I was praying, the Spirit of the Lord showed me *the word of God's wisdom*. He showed me what He wanted me to do in the future.

He said He wanted me to buy a school bus for a certain pastor, who was over 700 miles away. He plainly showed me that it would come to pass *in the future*.

I said, "Okay, Lord, I will buy the bus" (God wanted it to be done in the future), and I went on about my business.

Several celebrities were supposed to be at the meeting, but they got all fouled up. Some showed up, and some didn't make it. The person who was supposed to speak in the afternoon didn't make it, and they asked me to speak. I wasn't supposed to be on the program; nevertheless, there I was sitting on the platform of Howard University in front of a *packed out room* of people. They were standing around the walls.

They were going to introduce me as soon as a certain group finished singing. All of a sudden, *the Spirit of prophecy* came upon me in the form of a vision. As I sat there on the stage, I was getting a message down in my belly. The Holy Ghost can give you a message down there when it is *prophecy in known words. Prophecy* is words in a known language, that you understand, flowing out of your innermost being and building the congregation up. I began to get a prophecy for that particular congregation.

Just remember: *if it is God, and His Spirit comes on you to do something in a public service, you can hold it.* If it is not the Lord, you can't hold it. I have sat on platforms for over an hour with the Spirit of prophecy just rolling on the inside of me, waiting for the first blank spot to come so I could give it out. If it is from God, you will sit still and wait. It won't leave. You must wait upon the Lord and wait for the right time.

(I saw in that vision what was going to happen to the earth, spiritually. Now, I didn't see everything that is going to happen to the earth, spiritually. And I did not know at that time why God showed me the vision. It wasn't until two years later, when my campus ministry started, that I began to see it. God showed me because He wanted me involved. He has given several other people the same vision.)

That day at Howard University, I was just sitting there, and streams of tears were running down my cheeks: it was so sweet. The Spirit of prophecy was still in me when the singers were finished. I stood up and gave out the prophecy. God told that University Board something in that prophecy.

There were so many riots on campus, and so many students who were so ruthless. But two of those boys on that campus got saved, and they had a burden for that campus. They were so filled with the Holy Ghost that they talked the officials into giving them a check for $2,000 to have *a Holy Ghost* meeting. They said, "If you give us the money, we will have *a Holy Ghost* meeting, and we will change this campus."

As far as I know, that has never been done in the history of the world before. Imagine, taking $2,000 out of a college treasury in order to have *a Holy Ghost meeting!*

Another Vision the Lord Gave Me

Some years ago, God showed me another vision. I saw it in the spirit. Way up in the sky, I saw a big shoot of wind, like a whirlwind. It was coming straight out through the air, and then I saw another one. I looked one way, and I saw another. I looked over the other way, and I saw another. Then I could see the world — the four corners of the world

— and that wind was like a whirlwind coming from all four corners.

The whirlwinds were coming towards each other. Then they met head-on in the sky! When they met, all the whirlwinds turned into one huge chute, as one; coming down to the earth. That was God's healing power for the human race: God's healing power for bodies and God's healing power for salvation.

There is something about the wind that God just works through. The Spirit of God is coming like that wind. You don't know where it comes from but it is there. The wind starts going, but where does it come from? It is like a mystery.

> **But we speak the wisdom of God in a mystery, even the hidden wisdom, which God ordained before the world unto our glory.**
>
> **1 Corinthians 2:7**

The word of wisdom is like a mystery: the deep things of God are like a mystery to you. As you sit in your chair, reading this book, you may receive something from God. Or you may be riding in your car and receive *a word of wisdom*. One manifestation of the Holy Ghost may not last over 30 seconds. The Spirit of God may show you something. But if you don't pray about it, walk softly; you could miss God, and it would cause you all kinds of trouble. He can show you the same thing about a business.

That day, on the stage, God said to me, "This is the way, son, that the revival is coming to the earth; coming to the earth. Revival is coming to the earth. But it is going to come in the future — in the future. It is going to come mainly among the young people. I didn't say, '*totally*'; I said, '*mainly* among the young people.' "

The rest of the team members do not have the same vision that God gave me. Because the Lord showed me some

41

years ago how it was going to come. The only way that they will have the same vision is for God to give it to them supernaturally.

The revival is coming on the college campuses. Just get that through your head. I'm not talking about passing out tracts. I don't mean talking to a few students today and a few more tomorrow. I am telling you, revival is coming to the college campuses in this country. You may as well get ready!

You may ask, "Well, when will it come?"

I don't know anything about that. God may have me passing out tracts, and giving out books, and doing this and that five years from now. I don't know when, but mark it down — *revival is coming.*

You may be attending a meeting, and it will be twenty times as big on the campus of the University of Georgia: on Georgia Tech. Jesus will be baptizing students with the Holy Ghost all over the place. He will be healing them, and meeting their needs. You will start hearing about it happening on different campuses.

We are only getting a little taste of it right now, but I can see it! It is like the springs; like the water falling: it is like the dew dripping down. A prayer group here, a prayer group there, prayer groups on different college campuses. It is coming. I know, because God gave me a vision of *the word of wisdom;* it is going to happen in the future!

Stand Steadfast

The word of wisdom is a gift that is given to you by the Holy Spirit. It is a gift to *the Church* — *the Body of Christ,* and you are entitled to it. When it comes to you, *stand steadfast,* just as you do for a healing, and it will come to pass.

The *gift of the word of wisdom* may come to you quickly: it may be a few days; it may be a few weeks; it may take months, or possibly a few years. But you can know this, when the word of wisdom is imparted to you by the Holy Spirit, He is showing you something that is going to take place in the future. God wants you to have the wisdom in order to handle it.

Many Christians make the mistake of trying to rush God into doing things. God has His own timing.

It was about six or seven months after my stay in the Catholic priest's house (where God had told me to buy a certain pastor a school bus), when Dr. Lester Sumrall asked me to hold a meeting for him in South Bend, Indiana. A few months later, I went to South Bend.

Dr. Sumrall took me upstairs in his own house to a room. He told me that this was where I was going to stay. He told me to make myself at home, and that the people were going to enjoy my being there. He asked me to let him know if I needed anything.

After Dr. Sumrall left me alone in the room, I felt a chill. (When I stay in someone's home, I always kneel down and ask God to bless that home and all the people in it. I also ask the Lord if He wants to reveal anything to me for them that will encourage and bless them. And I tell Him that I will do it. I always want it to be from the Lord. I don't want to get mixed up in family problems. I always pray, "If anybody is going to get messed up in the future, just feel free to use me, Lord. I am available."

There have been many times when God would show me something and I have walked up to one of the mates and told them what God said. They would begin to cry. I have said, "Now listen, you are not being fair to your husband. The Spirit of God wants me to talk to you." I haven't had a single person yet who hasn't accepted what the Lord gave me through a word of wisdom for them.)

As I knelt down and prayed, "God, bless Brother Sumrall. Bless his home and bless the people here, Jesus. And Lord, just make me a blessing while I am here." As I was praying a word of the Lord came to me saying, "I want you to buy that pastor a school bus."

I said, "Yes, I know You do. You told me that eight or ten months ago in Washington, D.C. in that Catholic priest's home. I remember what You told me. Jesus, I don't know which school bus You want me to buy. I can't be more honest with You. I am willing to buy that school bus, but I am also going to tell You that I am not going to buy a school bus until You tell me which school bus You want me to buy. When You show me the school bus You want me to buy, then I will buy it.... I might go ahead and buy a used school bus, and You wanted me to buy a new one. Or I might go out and buy a new one when You want me to buy a used one. You show me the kind of school bus You want me to buy and I will buy it. Thank You, Lord."

Let us learn this about God: He respects honesty.

I owned the Yellow Cab Company in the city where I live. I used to get on my knees and pray, "Oh Lord, help me to sell this flaky company. I don't want the Yellow Cab Company. Do You hear me? Please send me a buyer."

He did not send a buyer. I called all the drivers in (there were about eight or ten drivers) when I first bought the company, and said, "Now listen men. I don't fool around with girls, prostitutes, and whiskey. I know that is how a lot of you guys make your living. I don't make money that way. I don't make my money crooked. The first driver that I find fooling with girls or whiskey, I am going to fire you. I am not going to tell you twice. I am telling you right now, and that is it. So — if that is what you are doing on the side, I am warning you right now, you had better stop it. Don't think that because you got away with it in the past that you can trick me. You may trick me for a while, but I will catch you. The Holy Ghost will show me.''

I caught one of them and I fired him. I think I liked him the best. I kept the company for eight years and had 24-hour service, 7 days a week. I wanted to stop Sunday service, but many elderly people needed cabs to get to church. I decided that if I stopped this flaky company from Sunday service those people couldn't get to church.

Finally I decided to close down on Sunday afternoons, after church. That was hard to do. Cab companies are important to a city. The mayor and the city council wanted it to operate 24 hours a day, 7 days a week for emergencies and the like. You may go for ten years and never need a cab, then suddenly at three o'clock in the morning you will need one.

It is always a good thing to have a taxi-cab company in a city. There was another cab company in town, and we went into partnership together. The other owner was an ex-sheriff of the town. One day, as time went on, we discussed dissolving partnership. I said that we could do it on a give and take basis. He drew up a contract that said he would pay me so much, and I couldn't start another cab company in Cleveland, Tennessee for ten years. I signed the contract. He paid me the amount we had agreed on, and I went down to the bank to deposit the money.

Now it was God's time.

As I stepped up to the teller's window, I saw the pastor God had told me to buy a school bus for. I said, ''Hi, Pastor!''

He stepped over to me and said, ''Where in the world have you been, Brother Norvel? Where has the good Lord taken you since the last time I saw you?''

I said, ''All over.''

He said, ''I don't doubt that!''

"Well — uh...."

He interrupted. "You know, I was down the highway, and was going to see the banker tomorrow when, all of a sudden, the Spirit of the Lord came upon me and told me to go to the bank this afternoon. So I got into my car and came up here."

I said, "What did you come up here for?"

He said, "Cleveland State College is over here. They have a school bus that they want to sell. They are taking bids on it. The highest bidder will get the bus. I just put in a bid, and when they opened up the box, where the bids were placed, my envelope was the only one in there."

By this time, the Holy Ghost was just causing my insides to jump up and down, saying, "This is the bus! This is the bus!"

I remembered my prayer in Lester Sumrall's bedroom, when I said, "Now Jesus, I am not going to buy a bus until You show me the one that You want me to buy, and I will buy it, You know."

I heard the Lord telling me, "That is what you said."

I said, "Yes, Lord. You are right."

I turned to the pastor and said, "Well, Pastor! Glory to God. I am glad to get this off my mind!"

"Get what off your mind?" he asked.

I said, "The bus...the bus! You wouldn't understand, Pastor. But you don't have to see any banker. Just trust me."

Of course he knew me real well. We had been together many times before. He said, "I won't do anything until you tell me what you want me to do."

I said, "Come get into my car and we will go to my office." We arrived at my office and I told my secretary to write the pastor out a check for the amount of the bus.

God had given me *a word of wisdom* many months before. Something was *to be done in the future.* And that was the time for it to come to pass.

For to one is given by the Spirit the word of wisdom...

1 Corinthians 12:8

Has the Spirit of God been dealing with you and you didn't even know what it was?

I can tell you right now what it is. It's a word of wisdom from God if He's showing you something that's going to come to pass in the future. It's a word of God's knowledge for you, to let you know. And you're involved in it. You might as well get ready.

If God has shown you something, but you didn't know what it was until now, and you want to yield yourself to God and say, "I'll do it," tell Him.

Prayer

Say: *"Jesus, I believe in the gifts of the Spirit. I believe in the word of wisdom. I believe the word of wisdom is a word of God's knowledge coming to me and letting me know something that God wants to come to pass.*

"I ask You, Jesus, to help me.

"I remember that thing that the Lord's been dealing with me about. I remember, Jesus, when You spoke it to me. I give myself to You, totally. I am available to carry that out, any time You want to bring it to pass.

"Thank You, Lord, for giving me a word of wisdom so that I won't be deceived, but I can go and carry out the work that the Spirit of God wants me to carry out.

"I love You, Jesus. I praise You, Jesus. I love the twelfth chapter of First Corinthians. I thank You for the gifts of the Spirit given to me as the Spirit wills. Thank You, Lord."

3

The Word of Knowledge

What is the gift of the word of knowledge? It is a part of God's knowledge, *a supernatural manifestation from heaven to a believer,* that comes into us. It lets us in on information and shows us things the way they are *right now*. It deals with facts.

It is not the word of wisdom. The word of wisdom points toward the future.

Every one of the nine gifts of the Holy Spirit has its own place. Not one of the other eight gifts can take care of the word of knowledge.

If you listen to God and be open and believe that the gift of the word of knowledge is for you, God will let you know the condition of things right now. The word of knowledge doesn't change things for you. You have to learn how to change them. And if you don't like the way things are, you can change them totally — that is, if you know how. Most believers, I'm sorry to say, don't know how.

Although I am not teaching on this here, I will pass on this information: If the condition is something bad, break the power of the Devil. Dedicate yourself to God, claim victory in English, then start praying in tongues until the note of victory comes (you'll know your prayer's been answered).

In other words, when God's power shows you the condition of something, the word of knowledge is being manifested to a believer. If you know how to change the condition, then you can teach somebody else how to change it.

How do you change something that's being destroyed into bright and glorious victory?

First of all, if damage is coming as a result of that thing, break the power of the Devil over it.

"The Lord will break it for me, won't He?" you may ask.

No, He won't break it. *You* break it. You use Jesus' name yourself. You're a member of God's Church. God gave His Son's name over to the Church to use to take authority over the Devil. You break the power of the Devil yourself, then claim victory. You have to say victory from your mouth: victory, victory, *victory!* Then pray in tongues.

"You mean pray in tongues until you *see* the victory?"

Not necessarily. It could happen that way. Pray in tongues until you see victory or until you get a note of victory.

"How long will it take?"

It might take three or four hours. It might take five or six hours. It took me eight hours one time.

I Stayed with It

The gift of the word of knowledge came to me supernaturally in a shopping center in Cleveland, Tennessee. The Holy Spirit said, "Go to Chattanooga, to a certain place."

So I took off down the highway. When I got to the place, there was a demon-possessed boy who had lost his mind. He had been out streaking, running around with no clothes on, and his mind had snapped. He didn't even know his own name. His daddy was on the way from New Jersey to see him.

A word of God's knowledge came and told me to go there — that's all. God didn't *show* me what was there, and He didn't *tell* me what was there. He could have if He'd wanted to, but He didn't want to.

You might say, "When God comes to you, why doesn't He tell you more about it?"

He doesn't want to.

"Why doesn't He want to?"

Because He's a faith God. He expects you to move into Him and get victory *by faith*. When He gives you a few words, you move by faith, and He gives you some more. You have to move with Him *by faith*. Sometimes that's easier said than done — especially if He tells you to go across the country.

If Jesus would say, "Go across the country," most people would ask, "What for?" I can tell you now, most of the time He's not going to tell them. It's none of their business.

That's the reason perhaps you didn't take some of those trips you were supposed to take, because you wanted to know what for. If God wanted you to know what for, He'd have told you. He didn't, so just forget it. You'll know soon enough — I'll guarantee you that. You'll know when you get there.

I will tell you this: If you'll go when God's word of knowledge tells you to go and do what God's word tells you to do, you have never been blessed yet like you'll be blessed. Just follow the instructions of the word of knowledge that come down from heaven to you. Not only will you be blessed, other people will be blessed mightily.

You've got to listen to what the Holy Ghost is saying to you. He knows exactly what's going on.

I prayed for the boy that was demon possessed for eight hours. I just broke the power of the Devil. I said, "Look, thief, (you have to call the Devil a thief if you believe he is one), you stole that boy's mind away from him, but you can't have it. Jesus has sent me here to get it back. I came here to stand in the gap for him, to get his mind back. I'm telling you, Satan, I came to take it away from you.''

After eight hours, the foam began to run out of the boy's mouth and his mind snapped back into him. I was determined. God had sent me there under the power of the manifestation of the Holy Spirit that lives inside of me, under the gift of the word of knowledge.

God imparted His knowledge to me to do something for Him right then — to go somewhere for Him *right then*! That's a weapon. That's what the word of knowledge is for: *it's a weapon of your warfare against the power of the Devil.*

You Need the Gifts of the Spirit

Let's read that seventh verse of the twelfth chapter of First Corinthians again:

> **But the manifestation of the Spirit is given to every man to profit withal.**

Don't read this and think, *I'm not worthy. God wouldn't give me the word of His knowledge. I'm just a little old nothing.*

Don't let the Devil beat you down into the ground. You have just as much right to the word of God's knowledge as anybody. Do you understand that? You have the Holy Ghost in you, and you have a right. God said that the manifestation of the Spirit is given to *every man* **to profit withal** (every man means every woman, too). You can miss God and miss Him big if you don't listen to the word of God's knowledge. Don't think, ''Oh, I'm a Christian. I love God, and Jesus sometimes heals people through me. I have a good relationship with the Lord. I don't necessarily *need* a word of God's knowledge. I can read the Bible and find out what God wants me to do.''

God says to you in verse 21, **And the eye cannot say unto the hand, I have no need of thee: nor again the head to the feet, I have no need of you.**

God made you. You're a human being. You belong to God and need every one of the nine gifts of the Spirit. In fact, whether you know it or not, you're desperate for them.

You may not feel that you're desperate for them right now, but you're going to be. There's going to come a time and place that you're going to need every one of the nine gifts of the Spirit. They all hold a unique place of their own from God in manifestation to you to bring you success. One can't take care of the other one, even though some of them are close and operate together.

Obey Quickly

One day, a word of God's knowledge came to a pastor's wife in Georgia. She worked for the governor of Georgia, and a word of knowledge came to her at work saying, "Call Norvel Hayes. I want him to come to your church and hold a meeting for a week or more."

She said, "Yeah, I've heard some of our members talk about him. They've heard him speak somewhere." She got home and told her husband.

He said, "I've never met Norvel Hayes. I don't know him."

"Some of our members do," she said. "Let's find out where he lives."

So they found out and called my office. I wasn't in, of course. I'm hardly ever there. So they talked to my secretary. They explained to her that a word of God's knowledge had come to them telling them that their church needed Norvel Hayes, right now.

When I came in, my secretary told me about it. When they got in contact with me, the Spirit of God said to me, "Go quickly!"

I said, "Yes, Sir."

I didn't know the pastor and I didn't know the church, but the Lord said, "Go." I went to the North Georgia mountains. They had a tiny church on a gravel road. Talk about back in the boondocks. I had a hard time finding the place. I don't mean it was off on some gravel road — it was *way out* on some gravel road.

When I went in, all of these mountain people were sitting in there singing songs already. As I went in, the Lord said, "Pray."

The pastor came down and said, "Are you Norvel Hayes?"

I said, "Yes, I am. Do you have some place where I can pray?"

He showed me to a room right off the main room. I went in there, knelt down, and started to pray. The Spirit of God fell on me supernaturally. I was on my knees crying and praying. The word of God's knowledge came unto me saying, "Get up and go out there and walk back and forth across the front of the church, and do it right now."

I was sobbing and crying, and I got up and just plowed my way through the door. I went outside and began to walk back and forth across the front of the church, crying and wringing my hands with the Spirit of God all over me.

After I walked for a little while, the power of God fell on the congregation and they began to shout all over the church, everywhere, just shouting and praising God.

They wanted me to stay over for a second week. I told them that I'd let them know on Friday night (that would have been the last service). On Friday morning as I was praying, a word of God's knowledge came unto me and said, "Stay here for another week."

I told the pastor, "God said stay." So I stayed.

One night, as I was at the altar, just praying for the people, the word of God's knowledge came unto me saying, "Go back to the city tomorrow and close the deal on that property."

I said, "Property? Property? Oh, yeah, yes Lord." I wasn't even thinking about property.

The sum of it was that I got up early the next morning and made my way to the lawyer's office. We drew up the papers and closed the deal on some property. I bought 444 acres of property in the mountains at a few hundred thousand dollars profit.

"Where'd you get it?"

I got it in a little mountain church on a gravel road in the North Georgia mountains where I was praying for people, getting them filled with the Holy Ghost and casting out devils.

What if I had not been receptive to the word of knowledge of God and obeyed Him?

You might say, "I wish God would bless me with $200,000."

Have you been to the North Georgia mountains yet?

"No, and I'm not going either."

The Holy Ghost can't do much for you then, because you're too ignorant. Any man that doesn't listen to the Spirit of God just has to wind up working his own things out.

They needed me in those Georgia mountains. God used me there, mightily.

The word of God's knowledge comes to you to tell you exactly what to do. You have to listen to Him. *Do it now! Don't put it off until next year.*

The Lord said to put the gospel first, and all these things shall be added unto you.

The Gift of the Word of Knowledge in the Bible

I think the greatest Old Testament example of the word of knowledge operating through a person is in the life of Elisha. It probably operated through him stronger than anybody else that I know of.

The king of the Syrians had declared war on the king of Israel. Elisha was in the land. God would give Elisha *a word of knowledge* to tell the king of Israel where the enemy army was going to camp that night.

Elisha would say, "Don't go that way, the enemy army is going to camp there, and they'll kill all of you."

The king of Israel would send somebody over there after Elisha had told them, and there they were!

Finally, it got to the point that God would impart a word of His knowledge to Elisha, telling him what the Syrian king would say in his bedroom.

Read this carefully: The gift of the word of God's knowledge is available for you! You'll be surprised at the things the Lord will let you know the condition of right now through a word of God's knowledge, if you'll only believe that. You have to believe it, though. You have to yield yourself to it.

"To what?"

To the Holy Ghost. You can't *make* God do it. It comes to you *as the Spirit wills.*

Let's read this account from 2 Kings 6:8:

> **Then the king of Syria warred against Israel, and took counsel with his servants, saying, In such and such a place shall be my camp.**

He'd tell his servants that. How in the world would Elisha know it? He was on the other side. He was with Israel. He knew it because *a word of God's knowledge* came unto him and told him.

> **And the man of God sent unto the king of Israel, saying, Beware that thou pass not such a place; for thither the Syrians**

are come down. And the king of Israel sent to the place which the man of God told him and warned him of, and saved himself there, not once nor twice.

Therefore the heart of the king of Syria was sore troubled for this thing; and he called his servants, and said unto them, Will ye not shew me which of us is for the king of Israel? And one of his servants said, None, my lord, O king: but Elisha, the prophet that is in Israel, telleth the king of Israel the words that thou speakest in thy bedchamber.

2 Kings 6:9-12

Do you see how strongly the word of knowledge operated in Elisha's life?

Let's look now at the life of Peter and see how this gift operated through him in Acts 10.

There was a certain man in Caesarea called Cornelius, a centurion of the band called the Italian band.

A devout man, and one that feared God with all his house, which gave much alms to the people, and prayed to God alway.

He saw in a vision evidently about the ninth hour of the day an angel of God coming to him, and saying unto him, Cornelius.

And when he looked on him, he was afraid, and said, What is it, Lord? And he said unto him, Thy prayers and thine alms are come up for a memorial before God.

Acts 10:1-4

Remember, Cornelius wasn't even saved, but he prayed every day. God sent an angel to Cornelius' house at the time of prayer. The angel said, in other words, "I have been sent from the Most High God unto you because your prayers, and your giving heart have been boiling into the throne of God. God has found favor with your prayers and with your giving, and with the love that you have for people in need."

And now send men to Joppa, and call for one Simon, whose surname is Peter:

> He lodgeth with one Simon a tanner, whose house is by the sea side: he shall tell thee what thou oughtest to do.
>
> And when the angel which spake unto Cornelius was departed, he called two of his household servants, and a devout soldier of them that waited on him continually;
>
> And when he had declared all these things unto them, he sent them to Joppa.
>
> Acts 10:5-8

Cornelius obeyed the word of the Lord that came through the angel.

Somebody may ask, "Why didn't the angel tell him how to get saved?"

God doesn't save people through angels, He saves people through *people*.

The word of God's knowledge came to Peter because he prayed. The Spirit of God told him to go pray, so he did. While he was praying, he saw a vision. Then he sat there, thinking on the vision. Now look at this: the word of God's knowledge came to Peter.

> While Peter thought on the vision, the Spirit said unto him, Behold, three men seek thee.
>
> Arise therefore, and get thee down, and go with them, doubting nothing: for I have sent them.
>
> Then Peter went down to the men which were sent unto him from Cornelius; and said, Behold, I am he whom ye seek: what is the cause wherefore ye are come?
>
> Acts 10:19-21

Did you see what Peter asked them? "Wherefore are ye come?" In other words, "I am the one you seek. What do you want?"

You might ask, "Why didn't God show him?" He didn't want to. He wanted Peter to act by faith and go on.

So Peter went with them to the house of Cornelius. He got there and opened up his mouth and started talking about Jesus.

> While Peter yet spake these words, the Holy Ghost fell on all them which heard the word.
>
> And they of the circumcision which believed were astonished, as many as came with Peter, because that on the Gentiles also was poured out the gift of the Holy Ghost.
>
> For they heard them speak with tongues, and magnify God....
>
> Acts 10:44-46

The Holy Ghost fell on the whole bunch of them. They were all saved, baptized in the Holy Ghost, and spoke in tongues just like on the day of Pentecost.

Peter was obedient to the word of knowledge. But the word of God's knowledge will not *make you do something*. God only *shares* a word of His knowledge with you. You don't have to obey it. But I'll guarantee you, if you will obey it, the greatest blessings that you've ever had in your life will result from it. It may come while you're there, or it may come later on. But I guarantee you, it will come if you obey the word of God's knowledge telling you the condition of something right now. God in heaven will pour out His blessings upon you.

What Is It For?

The Holy Ghost will give you a word of God's knowledge as the Spirit wills. It's for all kinds of things.

One day, one of my restaurants was about to get robbed, and the Spirit willed. At 5:00 in the morning God woke me up and brought that restaurant before me, and my spirit became grieved. The Lord said, *"Beware,* today, of that one restaurant of yours. Danger!"

That day the restaurant was robbed and the Lord let me see the man who robbed it. Glory be to Jesus! At 5:00 in the morning, He woke me up and brought it before me. That's what the word of knowledge is for: *to show you what's going to happen today, right now.*

One night, a few years ago, in Cleveland, Tennessee, I went into one of my restaurants for pizza with my date. When we got through eating the pizza, we walked outside and got into the car. I was going to take her home.

We had just walked a little way when all of a sudden the word of God's knowledge came unto me saying, "Beware, tonight, beware. Danger before you."

I jumped when the Holy Ghost did that to me. I said, "Look everywhere. Look outside. Look back. Look front. God said beware; danger before us."

She said, "Oh, okay."

I told her, "A word of God's knowledge came unto me, and He said, 'Beware, danger is going to happen, right now. Beware.' "

"You know, Norvel," she said, "you're something else."

We went about a mile when a car pulled out from behind some bushes and got right on my bumper. The Lord said, "That's it."

I said, "That's it. There's a man back there with a gun in the car."

The police in our town had been trying to get me to carry a gun for years, and I wouldn't do it. I said, "I don't want to carry a gun. I'll just trust the Holy Ghost."

The Lord showed me exactly what to do.

The man's car was very close to mine. In fact, his headlights were almost touching my bumper. I turned right to go to my date's house. She lived on a dead-end street. The other car pulled off and turned his lights out. That guy knew I was going to take her home. He knew exactly where I was.

And the Holy Ghost knew where he was, too! The Holy Ghost knew what tree he was parked behind; that's the reason the Holy Ghost said to me, "Beware." A word of

God's knowledge came unto me to save me out of that mess I could have gotten into.

A word of God's knowledge coming to you will let you know exactly what to do.

I pulled my car up in her driveway. We went in the house, and I called the police. They came straight to the house.

He thought I'd just let her out and come right back, but I didn't. God showed me what to do: go into the house quickly and call the police. I did, and they came.

They wouldn't even let me go. The police said, "Mr. Hayes, we're going to go home with you. You know we tried to warn you before. We'd like to give you a gun to carry." They went home with me and looked around the house.

A word of God's knowledge can save you. He'll let you know the condition of something right now, this very minute. He'll show you exactly as it is, not like you think it *might* be. He'll show you exactly like it is.

Get Out, Run

One night in Columbus, Ohio, I had just left a Billy Graham meeting. A word of God's knowledge came unto me as I was driving down the street. The Spirit of God came upon me and I had to park the car. The Lord said, "Pray." He showed me the condition of a Christian girl that lived in my hometown. She was going to go into a dark cloud. I could see her face. That lasted for about 15 minutes.

When I went back to my hometown, I wasn't going to tell her that the Holy Ghost had said, "Beware, don't do what you're going to do. You're in trouble now. Get out, run."

I didn't go the first day and tell her. The next morning when I opened my eyes, my body was hurting so badly,

I couldn't get out of bed. God wanted me to go and minister to her, to tell her that the word of knowledge came unto me saying, "Beware and run."

I finally got my clothes on and pulled my way down the steps. I had to hold onto the car to get into it. I finally got to this girl's apartment. I pulled my way up the steps and knocked on the door.

"Jeanie," I said, "I was in Columbus, Ohio, riding down West Broad Street and a word of God's knowledge came unto me. He brought you before me and said to tell you, '*beware*. You're being swept into a dark cloud. Beware, run, run, run!' What are you doing, Jeanie?"

"I'm not doing anything," she said. "What do you mean?"

"Jeanie, who are you dating?"

"I'm dating a boy that I met down at Daytona Beach, Florida, when I was on my vacation."

"Where did you meet him?"

"I met him down on the beach."

"What was he doing?"

"He was drinking beer."

"Jeanie, you're a Christian, and you love God. What are you dating him for? The hand of God is upon you. A word of God's knowledge came unto me to tell you to beware, Jeanie. Run, run, Jeanie. Run now."

"But, Norvel," she said, "How can I run? He's moved up here from Daytona Beach, and he's living here in Cleveland, Tennessee, now. I'm dating him steadily, and we're thinking about getting married. You haven't seen him, Norvel. He's so good looking."

I said, "The word of God's knowledge came unto me to tell you to run, Jeanie. Beware and run."

About the second or third time I told her, everything was fine. I felt just as light as a feather. I felt like I was about 16. I felt so good from the top of my head to the bottom of my feet, when I delivered exactly what God wanted me to deliver — a word of His knowledge to tell her exactly what to do.

"I've done my share, Jeanie," I said. "I'll see you, honey. But you better beware. You better run and run fast."

That was a word of God's knowledge trying to rescue one of His children. But the sad part of this story is that she didn't run. She was a little doll herself, and he was a real nice-looking young fellow. And they got married.

I was talking to a girl in the jewelry store one day, and I noticed a young fellow working there. I'd never seen him before. The girl asked me if I knew who he was. I said that I didn't.

"That's Jeanie's husband," she told me.

I said, "He's a nice-looking young fellow."

"Isn't he though? Do you know what he is?" she asked.

"No, I don't know what he is. I don't know anything about him."

"He's a gigolo from Daytona Beach. He lives off of old, rich women. He goes to bed with them to get their money. He's been a gigolo for several years. Do you see that black-haired girl standing out there looking in the window now? She acts like she's looking at jewelry, but that's his girlfriend."

I said, "Oh, God, no, not to Jeanie. Oh, Jesus, Jeanie is so sweet. Not to Jeanie."

But the sad part of it is, it was to Jeanie. But it was Jeanie's own fault. She didn't listen to a word of God's knowledge telling her the condition of things right now and telling her to beware and run.

I saw Jeanie live through five years of hell and heartaches. She had one child. Her husband would stay out all night with some other girl. She would lock him out of the apartment. She went through five years of that. She finally got sick of him. There was no decency about him. So she left with her little four-year-old girl.

I saw that girl live several years of agony, in torment and hell, because she overrode the word of knowledge.

She told me, "Norvel, I've thought about you so much. I've wanted to talk to you so many lonely, disturbed, confusing nights. I would say, 'Jesus, if I could just talk to Norvel, and let him pray for me or something.' "

But God didn't deal with me to talk to her anymore. God never told me she was lonely. God used me to give her a word of knowledge not to do it, and she overrode that. She suffered a living hell for several years because of it, but there wasn't any need for it. God didn't want her to.

God doesn't want you to suffer a living hell over several years. *And you don't have to if you'll listen to a word of God's knowledge.* It comes to you by the Holy Ghost that lives inside you. It could come to you yourself, or it could come to you through another person.

The gift of a word of knowledge is a revelation gift: God reveals and unfolds His will to you. If you're born again, and you have the Spirit of God in you, the Holy Ghost will give it to you. But you must treat it as a precious thing. If you don't keep it as a precious thing, it will stop operating. You have to show God respect for His manifestations.

Give Him Up

A pastor came to me one day and asked me to come with him to pick up his daughter at the college campus. I went with him at 3:00 in the afternoon. She got out of class, walked to the car, and got in the back seat. I was in the front seat with the pastor.

As we were going down the highway, all of a sudden, the Spirit of the Lord came upon me in the car. A word of God's knowledge came unto me and said, "Cry and make intercession for her and I will unfold to her."

The Holy Ghost began to cry through me, and I slumped over the dashboard. I began to cry and weep and weep. I cried and prayed all the way to the parsonage.

When we arrived at the parsonage, they got out of the car and went into the house. I sat out there in the car and cried and prayed for an hour.

All of a sudden, the Spirit of the Lord went into the girl's bedroom and hit her like a bolt of lightning. She came out of the house screaming. She ran and jumped into the car where I'd been praying. She grabbed the steering wheel and started screaming, "I don't want to give him up. I don't want to give him up."

"It doesn't make any difference what you want, you had better."

"Okay, Norvel, okay," she said.

She just cut him off all of a sudden. She wouldn't date him. She told me that he nearly went nuts. He almost had gotten her into bed the night before that. She was so close. But the Holy Ghost came by the word of knowledge to tell her what to do. And she obeyed that. She wouldn't go out with him for 12 months.

I thought it was all settled. I thought she had listened to God. A year went by, and she wouldn't even go out with him. Then I heard she was dating him again. It wasn't very long until they were married.

When she was a little child, she was called by God to be a missionary. She had never been to a movie in her life. Now they go to sex movies. A missionary ministry was shot down the drain because she wouldn't listen to a word of God's knowledge.

You better listen when God speaks to you, brother and sister. If you don't, you've got a lot of years of hell to live in.

The gifts of the Holy Spirit in the twelfth chapter of First Corinthians are God's weapons against the Devil. They are God's weapons for the warfare you're in. The Devil and all the demons from hell can't pull a bunch of dumb tricks on you if you listen to the Holy Ghost.

When God speaks — listen!

Prayer

If you want God to show you the condition of things right now, the way they are, you have to yield yourself to the Holy Spirit. You have to be available for the Holy Spirit to use you as He wills.

Say: *Thank You, Jesus for the twelfth chapter of First Corinthians. I don't know everything, but You do, Jesus. Thank You, Jesus, for a word of God's knowledge coming to me. It's a gift of the Spirit, given to me freely when I need it, as the Spirit wills. Help me, Jesus, to yield myself to the revelation knowledge of God. Thank You, Lord. I receive, in Jesus' name.*

4
The Gift of Faith

If you are a believer and have been baptized in the Holy Ghost, all of the nine gifts of the Spirit should be operating through you. And they will be, if you know how to listen to the Holy Spirit and learn what He's trying to get across to you. The gifts of the Spirit are so important.

What are the gifts of the Spirit anyway? *They are God's spiritual weapons that He's given to the Church.*

Now remember, God is a Spirit. The Devil is a spirit. You are living on the earth where the Holy Spirit and the Devil live. But this world has been turned over to the Devil. He took it over because man would not listen to God. Rebellion against God caused the Devil to take it over.

Since that time, if you are going to get any information from heaven, it's got to be through the Word and the Spirit. Listen to God. He is talking to you.

Don't Be Ignorant

Now concerning spiritual gifts, brethren, I would not have you ignorant.

1 Corinthians 12:1

God doesn't want you to be ignorant of the gifts of the Spirit. You might say, "They don't all operate through me. Why don't I have them?"

It's because you're ignorant of them. Now, I didn't say you were an ignorant person. I said *you are ignorant of the gifts.* You don't understand how they operate.

You might say, "Why don't they operate through me?" Because you haven't been taught about them.

Ye know that ye were Gentiles, carried away unto these dumb idols, even as ye were led.

verse 2

The reason the gifts of the Spirit don't operate and aren't given out through very many churches, is because they don't believe in the gifts. When the churches start teaching on it, preaching on it, and believing it, then it will come into manifestation. It will be given out by the Holy Ghost that lives inside of them.

You can't fight the Bible and get God to give you anything. The Holy Ghost does in the congregation what goes out from behind the pulpit.

Remember...**the manifestation of the Spirit is given to every man to profit withal** (v. 7).

And "every man" includes you!

You can have it if you want it. You have to believe it.

I want you to get it inside of you solid and strong that every one of the gifts of the Spirit is just as important as the others when that particular gift is needed. Every one of the gifts of the Spirit is a matter of life and death on a particular day for you in your life in a particular situation.

Different Kinds of Faith

There are three power gifts: the gift of faith, the gifts of healing, and the gift of working of miracles.

Now faith is the substance of things hoped for, the evidence of things not seen.

Hebrews 11:1

This verse is talking about regular faith, the Hebrews-kind of faith, *not the gift of faith.*

I know a woman, a good friend of mine, who is a pastor's wife, and yet she was dying of cancer 25 years ago. Jesus walked into her room and healed her. She has been healed ever since. The Devil's been trying to give her cancer for 25 years. She won't receive it. Symptoms of cancer come back, but she has faith enough in God's Word that she will get flat on the floor and pray herself through doubt and unbelief and the smog and fog from hell.

Every six months or so the Devil will come and try to kill her with cancer, but she won't receive it. She prays until everything leaves her. She prays herself into the glory of God. She prays until God's healing power comes down and surges through her, removing all symptoms from her. She prays until that happens. That is what you call *Hebrews-kind of faith — you believe that God means what He says.* Right now! Faith is the substance! She believes that her faith is the substance to health. You can learn to do that on your own. But that is not the gift of faith.

There are all kinds of faith. Let me point out some other kinds of faith to you.

A farmer has faith. He sows his seed and believes it is going to come up. That is faith.

You exercise faith every time you walk across a busy street expecting the cars to stop for a red light.

You show faith when you put your money in the bank. You have faith in the honesty and integrity of the bank officers.

Why don't you have the same kind of faith in God's Word?

Bible Examples of the Gift of Faith in Manifestation

The gift of faith is a *gift of power.* I want you to understand how the gift of power works and why God will give it to you.

God gives a believer a gift of power because there is something that He wants to do. It is always to bless somebody or help somebody. Or, God can give a believer a gift of power to stop something that is evil.

Let me point out a couple of Bible men that had the gift of faith operating through them. These are in the Old Testament.

Daniel had the gift of faith operating in his life. He was a man of God. (See Dan. 6.) When they put him in the lions' den, he was thoroughly convinced that the lions would not bite him. Of course, in the morning he was still there. The angel had come and shut the lions' mouths. God's power came and he knew it. He had the faith. He wasn't a nervous wreck when he went in there.

The gift of faith came upon Samson. He had more power than any human being recorded in the Bible. But God gave it to Samson *when he needed it.* (Judges 15:14-15.) A whole army was going to get him; but he just killed the whole bunch by himself, hundreds of them, with the jawbone of a donkey. Brother, that's power! He had more of God's power than anybody that I know of. But it was a gift of the Spirit.

When God sees that you are available, He will give you the gift of faith.

The gift of faith is a gift of power to get the job done in whatever situation you're in at that particular time. God doesn't give you *all* His power, and different times He gives you different amounts of power. *He only gives you the amount of power you need to get that job done.*

To Help Someone

Let me explain how the *gift of faith* operates through a believer's life. The first time it ever operated in my life was for the benefit of somebody else.

Who?

A Spirit-filled Christian woman, to keep her from dying.

This woman was sick in her stomach. Then she had trouble with her breathing. It kept getting worse. Her husband had to take her to Florida all the time. He had to keep her in Florida, six months sometimes, and let her sit out in the sun. It didn't help her stomach any, but it helped her breathing a little. She could live.

This woman and her husband were both Spirit-filled and loved God. I was scheduled to be the speaker at the FGBMFI chapter where the husband was an officer. The wife's name is Helen. She played the piano for conventions and things like that. God was wanting to use her mightily.

I spoke that night and then gave the invitation. She was one of the first ones in line to be prayed for. She came for healing. I prayed for her and for all the rest of them down the line. When I got through praying, I was just standing there. The Spirit of God was working with some of them. Some of them were praising the Lord. Some of them were walking back to their seats.

I looked up where she was sitting. She looked so sad. I didn't know what was happening to me, but the moment I looked on her, I began to see her healed. Power came on me! And I got mad at her. She should have been walking up and down the church, or at least sitting back in her seat saying, ''Thank God, I'm healed! Thank You, Jesus, I'm healed! Glory to God, I'm healed!'' But she wasn't. She was sitting there with her head down. She looked like she was getting ready to die. I never saw such a sad look on anybody's face.

I looked at her, and the power came on me. It was like everybody else in the place just disappeared from me. I knew they were there, but I couldn't care less. The gift of faith dropped on me, and I could not have cared less what anybody thought.

I walked over to her and said, ''*Helen!*''

She looked up at me.

I said, *"What are you going to do? sit here and let the Devil kill you? Why don't you rise up? I prayed for you in Jesus' name one time! That is all you need, Helen. Do you understand that? You are healed! By His stripes you are healed! Why don't you rise up, Helen? Let God heal you! Why don't you rise up?"*

While I was doing that, she was looking at me. I kept saying that for about 30 seconds.

All of a sudden she looked at me and said, *"Okay, Norvel! Okay!"*

The power came like the wind and left like the wind. The power wasn't on me anymore. God changed me so quickly, and he restored me back to my normal self just as quickly. It was like the bat of an eye.

Then, *the same power* that was on me, was on her. She was standing there screaming the victory just like I had been screaming at her. She was screaming, *"I'm healed!"*

I was standing there with no power. You know what happens, don't you, if you obey God? Immediately, in your mind (that is where the Devil operates—in your mind), the Devil starts in.

He said to me, "You're nuts! You're crazy! You're a fanatic! They'll never invite you to speak here again, you crazy thing! What are you screaming at that woman for like that? That's not nice." The Devil is cunning. He will come to you just so slick and smooth. That was my first time. I thought, "Oh, what did I do?"

The Devil said, "They will never invite you back here to speak. You have just closed the doors for your ministry, because this will get out all over the country. You've had it. You won't get any more invitations, you dummy! You crazy thing! You're getting too wild, you're supposed to be nice."

72

I thought, "Oh, God, what did I do?" I was ashamed to look at the people. But I did look at them. Some of them were looking at me and some at her.

She was still standing there screaming, *"I'm healed!"* *It went from me into her.* But I didn't know that until about a week later. There was a convention a week later not very far away. I thought I would go up one day, see who was speaking, and enjoy the service. I walked into the auditorium. There were several hundred people there. Helen was playing the piano.

When she saw me come in, she stopped playing the piano and jumped off the stage. She ran down the aisle to me, and said, "Brother Norvel, I'm healed. I'm healed completely. Everything has disappeared. I went out that night and ate a T-bone steak, and I digested it. It's the first time I've digested food in six months. I've eaten anything I've wanted to since that night, Brother Norvel. Everything has disappeared from me. I breathe real good, and my stomach is completely healed. Look at my face, I'm getting my color back. My cheeks are already turning rosy. I've gained about nine pounds since that night. Norvel, do you remember me? Do you remember that night, when you were screaming at me?"

I said, "Yeah, honey, I remember when I was screaming at you."

She said, "You probably don't know what happened. While you were screaming at me that power started coming from you and into me. That power that went into me caused me to be strong enough and bold enough to start confessing my healing — boldly. *When I started confessing my healing boldly, I got healed.* All the afflictions disappeared!"

The *gift of faith* is what did it. I know the gift of healing followed it when she started confessing her healing. But the gift of faith changed me into another person to make her think differently.

The gift of faith caused a woman who had been eating only baby food for six months to start eating normally and not die! God gave me the power to talk to her like that so she could start believing the Bible and rise up against that thing.

You have to rise up against the Devil.

I don't care what kind of works the Devil gives, you have to rise up against him!

To Stop the Works of Hell

God gave me great favor one time by the *gift of faith* operating through me.

I was speaking in a prison out at Canyon City, Colorado. I got up on the stage, and hundreds of prisoners came in. (I was going to speak to them first and eat with them afterwards.)

I got up there and started talking about Jesus, and they started laughing at me. I don't mean one or two of them, I mean they all started laughing and pointing at me. I just acted like I didn't see them. I had to shut my mind off from them, which is easier said than done. I just kept on and acted like I had a one-track mind. That lasted about 20 or 25 minutes, until God got tired of it. God gave them every chance in the world to shut up, but they didn't do it.

All of a sudden, power fell on me! *I'm talking about supernatural power.* I wasn't a regular Bible teacher anymore. I wasn't standing there anymore just speaking with authority and teaching the Bible. *Power came on me!* Glory to God! He changed me into another man.

I looked at them, straight in the face, and said, ''What are you fellows laughing at me for? I'm not in here. You're the ones who are in here, you dummies! I came in here to give you life, so you could go to heaven and live forever, and you're sitting there laughing and making fun and heckling. God doesn't like it. God knows where you are

74

sitting! He knows who you are! He knows exactly what happened to you! But you don't even know, you are so ignorant!

"Now you sitting there, you're so dumb you don't even know why you raped that woman. You're 24 years old and you raped a woman 60 years old. You don't even know why you did that! You got 64 years.

"You over here, you don't even know why you robbed that bank. You're sitting here with 25 years, and you're so dumb, you don't even know what made you rob the bank.

"You, why did you shoot that man? You don't even know why you shot that man! You're so ignorant, you don't even know why you're in here.

"Nearly every one of you sitting there like little lambs is thinking, *When I get out, I'm going to be better*. No, you're not going to be better, you evil hard-hearted rascal! You're going to be meaner! That same demon from hell that put you in here this time will put you in here again! The record says that 87 percent of you will come back again. I came to tell you how to stay out forever! Do you understand that? Now I want you to sit there and be quiet!"

I never heard another noise. I never heard another laugh or anything from the moment I first opened my mouth when God's power fell on me supernaturally.

I just kept on going for ten minutes. I guess I didn't teach anymore, I started preaching. God's power fell on me for about ten minutes. Then I said, "Bow your heads! I'm going to pray for you."

They bowed their heads.

"Jesus, I know You love these men! Touch their hearts. I ask You to do it. You don't want these men in this prison, Jesus. You didn't put them in here. You want them to be citizens. You want these boys that aren't married to get married. You don't want them to fool around with each other. You want them to get married to a girl, have children, have a family, be normal.''

As I was praying for them, God's power came in. They broke and started crying. The Lord just moved in there so strong.

I said, ''The state of Colorado won't allow me to give an invitation. I'd like to put my arms around each one of you and pray for you, but they won't let me. Everyone of you who knows you've done wrong, but you're not proud of it, and you believe Jesus is real and He loves you — everyone of you who'd like Jesus to show you He loves you, you'd like to give your life to Him, say yes to Him, and stop fighting Him — hold up your right hand.''

Hands began to go up all over the prison. I got them to repeat a sinner's prayer. I dismissed them.

I told them, ''I'm walking with you. We are going over to have some food together. If I can answer any of your questions, feel free to ask me.''

So, I talked to them as we went over. I have never been treated any nicer in my lifetime. When we got over there to eat, they had the highest respect for me. They treated me like their chaplain or something. Why? Because the gift of faith came upon me and gave me the power — the right amount of power I needed to get the job done, right then.

I had a good time with them. Many of the prisoners got saved and had a good time. They learned something that day. I guess they learned a little bit from me, but they learned mostly from the *gift of faith.*

To Set the Captives Free

The gift of faith will operate through you sometimes for a demon-possessed person, especially if he wants to be free. If he is crying out for help and wants to be free, it will operate through you. It did me one time.

A girl in our town, a Spirit-filled Christian girl, was hanging around with the wrong boys and started going to bed with them. She was raised as a Spirit-filled Christian. She knew better, but she got in so far that she couldn't get out. She'd tell herself every day, "I'm not going to bed with this boy tonight. I'm not going to." She'd go out, she'd say she wasn't going to, but she would wind up doing it — every night.

She started visiting churches, knocking on the church doors, and asking for help. You know how most pastors are — they're real nice — and they prayed for her. *But you don't pray for a demon-possessed person. You cast the devil out of them!*

I was planning to go to a convention, I think in Kansas City. The Lord let me know that He didn't want me to go to the convention. He wanted me to go to a prayer meeting Wednesday night. There were a few people there. The preacher preached and gave an invitation. This girl got up out of her seat and went down to the front altar. The Spirit of God said in me, "Go pray with her."

So I did. I got down on my knees beside her and prayed with her. She was crying out for help. She cried, "Help me, Jesus. Some way help me, Lord."

I thought to myself, "What's wrong with her?" I was praying, "Help her, Lord."

I was the only one up there praying. I prayed about 15 minutes, I think. Right towards the end when I was praying one or two more came up, knelt down around there, and started praying. I felt I didn't want to pray anymore. I got up off my knees and went back to my seat and sat down.

I was sitting there, minding my own business, and the Lord began to roll the sixteenth chapter of Mark around in front of me—the Great Commission.

> Go ye into all the world, and preach the gospel to every
> creature. He that believeth and is baptized shall be saved;
> but he that believeth not shall be damned. And these signs
> shall follow them that believe; In my name shall they cast
> out devils.
>
> Mark 16:15-17

"In my name shall they cast out devils."

I said, "Please, Lord Jesus, in this particular church,
I don't think they cast out devils."

"The sixteenth chapter of the book of Mark casts them out."

"Lord, I don't have enough power to do that," I said.
"Don't make me do that. I have friends here. Besides that,
Lord, I don't run this church. I don't think they do that in
here."

*"The sixteenth chapter of the book of Mark does. In My name
they shall cast out devils. Those that believe in Me, in My Name,
they shall cast out devils."*

"Yes, Lord, yes." I was crying by that time. He just
kept rolling it around in front of me, just like He had a one-
track mind. I wanted the Lord to get over in the book of
Matthew, or Luke, but He didn't go anywhere. He just
stayed in the sixteenth chapter of the book of Mark and the
Great Commission.

> These signs shall follow them that believe; In my name
> shall they cast out devils.
>
> Mark 16:17

"Yes, Lord, I know it's in there," I said. All the time
I was trying to talk to Him, He wasn't even listening.

After a while, I said, "Lord, I work for You."

*"I know you do. I hear you going around the country saying
that you love Me, you love Me, 'Oh, I love Jesus. Jesus has done
so much for me—let me tell you what He's done for me.' Tonight
I demand you show me!"*

Words are cheap. I already know what He wanted me
to do, but I was trying to get out of it.

He started melting me. He said, "Look at that girl at the altar, crying out for help. Look at her, son. She's crying out for help and nobody has helped her. She's been to church after church after church, and she's still crying out for help."

Jesus said, *"Look at her! I want to help her through you."* This got me—I absolutely couldn't take it.

He said to me just so plainly, *"It doesn't make any difference to Me now, the past is past. It doesn't make any difference to Me how many boys she's been to bed with. I love her, and she's crying out for Me. I love her, and I love all of those like her. If you are going to work for Me, you had better not forget that. I didn't put that evil spirit in her that makes her do the things she does. The Devil put it in her. The Devil has gotten in her. I want you to go up there and use My name, and cast that thing out of her."*

"Jesus," I said, "Lord, I'm not ashamed of You, Jesus."

"Show Me. If you are not ashamed of the sixteenth chapter of the book of Mark, you are not ashamed of Me. If you are ashamed to obey it, you are ashamed of Me. If you are not ashamed of Me, and you love Me, show Me. I love her. I want to help her."

I said, "Jesus, You have the power. I know You have the power. Go ahead and help her, Lord."

"I work through My Word. I work through believers. I'll do what you do. You obey the sixteenth chapter of the book of Mark, and I'll be with you."

Remember what Jesus told the disciples? He didn't say, "I'll go *before* you and do all the work." He said, "I'll go *with* you, confirming the Word with signs *following*."

"Give me power, Jesus," I said, "and I'll do it. I'll do anything You tell me to do, if You'll give me power." I meant business.

As soon as I said that, on the inside of my belly, the Holy Ghost began to rise up, like somebody blowing up a balloon. *The power began to come into me.* I had power in my fingers. I had power in my hands. I had power in my arms. I had power in my chest. My eyes were full of power. I couldn't see anything except victory! My mouth was full of power! *Everything about me was full of power.*

When the power came on me, I got up out of my seat! I walked down there like I was going to battle. As I got down there, a guy was standing close to her.

"Have her stand up because God is going to set her free!" I said.

He said, "Stand up, young lady, stand up."

I put my hand on the side of her head and said, *"You foul spirit that has wrecked this girl's life, in Jesus' name, come out of her!" I said it one time.* It was like the wind. It had to be a demon—*whoosh!* Her body went back through the air and hit the floor. She landed flat on her back. The moment she hit the floor, tears gushed out of her eyes, and she started speaking in tongues just as fast as she could.

The *gift of faith* made the difference. It gave me power to get the job done. The people all shouted and rejoiced and praised God.

Several months later that pastor called me. The girl was going to get married. "She wants you to read the Bible at her wedding," he said.

She was getting married in her house. The wedding started. She was in the other room. She came around the corner, marching to *Here Comes the Bride*. I looked and saw her. The Spirit of the Lord came upon me, and so softly and sweetly Jesus spoke to me. Tears were streaming down my cheeks. He said, "Thank you, son, for obeying the sixteenth chapter of the book of Mark and for casting the Devil out of her. Now she comes to be married, and she stands before Me, clean and white as snow. She stands before Me as an angel, as though she had never sinned." Glory be to God!

Can you imagine Jesus thanking me for doing something? You know what it means for Jesus to come to you and thank you? I want to thank Him for what He has done for me.

Oh, praise the blessed name of the Lord God forever because of the gift of faith!

To Bring Salvation

Some people called me from Philadelphia and wanted me to come to a business meeting. Between the sessions, they dismissed us to go eat. We walked into a restaurant, and we didn't have any reservations. We walked over to the dining room. When they said, "Table for two," the man who was doing the lecturing at the meeting and I just stepped out. We sat down at the table.

I'm a Christian businessman. It's just a normal thing to me to sit down and say, "Well, thank You, Jesus. Praise the Lord. Isn't Jesus good?"

The man looked at me and said, "Mr. Hayes, I want to tell you something. I don't believe in that kind of stuff."

"You don't believe in God?"

"No!"

"Why not?" I asked.

"People say that God is love."

"He is."

"Oh, yeah? My wife is an alcoholic, Mr. Hayes. I have a 12-year-old son and a 14-year-old son. My 14-year-old son is a dope addict. If God is love, He sure didn't stop at our house. Why should I believe in Him?"

I said, "You have to believe God. You have to show God faith that you believe in Him. God will give you whatever you want." Then I started giving my testimony, telling him what God had done for me. It was like water running off a duck's back. He didn't believe a word of it.

"It may be true, but I doubt it. It probably just turned out that way for you. I don't believe it."

He let me know it didn't even phase him. We finished eating. We were walking up the sidewalk to the meeting room. I was minding my own business, talking to him. Some of the other men were walking in front of us, and some were behind us.

All of a sudden, *power* fell on me and changed me into another man! God gave me words to say to him. When it happened to me, I wheeled around. I got him by the arm and pulled him around. I stuck my finger in his face and said, *"Listen, Mister, God's real regardless of what you believe! Jesus told me to tell you that He doesn't want your two sons to die and go to hell. If you don't introduce them to Him, when you die and go to hell, He's going to hold you responsible for them!"*

I just turned around and walked off. He stood there looking like I had hit him with a stick.

I went in and sat over against the wall. He came and sat at the desk, because he was the lecturer. I looked over at him and the *gift of faith* came upon me—*power* came upon me—again. This time it was a different type of manifestation. The first time on the sidewalk was *authority*. This time the Spirit of God began to move upon my innermost being, and I began to cry and weep. Compassion boiled up out of me. The power was all over me.

The Lord said to me, "Walk over there and pray for him, right now."

Some of the other men had come in and were sitting around. I just walked across the floor crying. I walked up to his desk. I said, "As I was sitting against the wall the Spirit of the Lord came upon me. Jesus loves you and He wants me to pray for you. Bow your head and close your eyes and I'm going to pray for you right now." I was crying. He looked up at me, and my hands were up.

He said, "Oh, oh, okay."

I reached up and touched him on the top of the head, and I said, *"Jesus, touch this man. Jesus, give this man another life. Touch him!"* His head fell down onto the desk like he'd been hit with a hammer. He started crying as soon as his head hit the desk—he started crying and weeping.

I said, "Tell Jesus you are sorry for your sin. Ask Jesus to come into your heart, Mister, right now. The Spirit of the Lord is all over you. Ask Him to come into your heart!"

He said, "Jesus, come into my heart." He just cried and wept and sobbed on the top of the desk. There he was. And five minutes before, he didn't believe in God.

You might say, "Norvel, that was a good job. You really did the right thing, didn't you?"

Are you kidding? I told him everything I knew, and it didn't phase him. My knowledge of God couldn't even get to him. *It was a gift of power that God gave that made the difference.*

A year later I was sitting on the stage in a FGBMFI convention in Phoenix, Arizona. I saw a guy walking up the aisle grinning from ear to ear. He jumped up on the stage where I was sitting. He walked over to me and said, "Brother Norvel, it's wonderful. God is wonderful. Jesus is wonderful."

"Yeah, I know He is. I know He's wonderful."

"Don't you remember me—Philadelphia, Pennsylvania?" he asked.

"Oh, dear Lord! Yeah, I remember you."

"Do you know what happened to me?"

"No."

"I went home to my alcoholic wife," he said. "I told her, 'I met this strange man. He put his hands on my head and something came in me and knocked me on the desk. I began to cry and weep.' I told her that I got saved. Then she got saved. I told my dope-addict son, and he got saved.

My son got filled with the Holy Ghost. I got filled with the Holy Ghost. My wife is here. My son is going to Bible school. All my relatives are saved. I moved from Philadelphia to California. I'm the president of a FGBMFI chapter in California now."

I said, "You mean all in one year?"

"It doesn't take me long to do something," he said.

See, God wanted to save him. You might say, "Why did God save him?"

Because I was available for the gift to operate through. The gift of faith came upon me! The power was on me. The power went from me into him when I touched him on the top of his head. The gift of faith can change people. The Spirit of God can change people through the gift of faith. But He has to have believers to operate through.

It's a supernatural gift! It's available for the Church. It's available for you—anybody!

But the gift of faith will never operate through you unless you make yourself available.

Prayer

Make yourself available to the Lord for the gift of faith.

Say, *"Jesus, I'm available for the gift of faith. I'm available to be changed into another person to help somebody, to bring healing to somebody, to bring salvation to somebody, to stop the evil works of the Devil, and to bring the glory of God into manifestation on the earth. I'm available for God's power to come upon me and change me. I'm available.*

"I love You, Jesus. I love the gospel. Mold me into the person You want me to be. I believe in First Corinthians 12. I believe the gift of faith is a gift of power that God gives to believers to get the job done. Thank You, Jesus, I'm free from unbelief."

5
The Gifts of Healings

One of the power gifts is called the *gifts of healings*. I know the *King James Version* of the Bible lists this as "gifts of healing" but, in the Greek, both words are plural — *gifts of healings*. *Why* is it plural? Because many things cause sickness.

Some sicknesses are caused by accidents, some by personal neglect. Some are caused by organic ailments, some by a spirit of infirmity or actual satanic oppression. Some sicknesses and diseases are caused by actual demon possession.

A gift of healing is God's power flowing down through your body to drive out afflictions in Jesus' name. It comes as the Spirit wills.

A gift of healing is a gift of power that God drops on people, but it's not manifested in the same way all the time. Sometimes God's healing power drops on you, and your body just unfolds before Him — you just drop on the floor. Sometimes it drips on you, and it comes so easy and precious and sweet and warm. Sometimes God's healing power will drop on you and you won't even *feel anything*. You have to check yourself and find out that you're healed.

When a gift of healing comes, it comes so quickly. It's given as the Spirit wills. You never know when it's going to happen.

There are all kinds of ways for you to be healed. Laying on of hands is one way to be healed.

A gift of healing works differently. It is still God's healing power. Don't get me wrong. It's the same *kind* of healing power that comes when a person lays his hands on somebody, but *it usually comes in a stronger way.*

Some people receive God's healing power and the gifts of healings and nobody touches them. They don't necessarily try to quote anything; it just comes to them automatically. That's involved in the gifts of healings that's given out as the Spirit wills (listed in 1 Corinthians chapter 12). When it comes, it just comes.

What is it?

It's an amount of power that God chooses to give as He manifests Himself.

You say, ''Why doesn't He give it to everybody who's sick?''

I don't know.

Kathryn Kuhlman said one time, ''When I get to heaven, I'm going to ask Jesus, 'Why do two wheelchair cases get up and walk off, and ten don't?' ''

I don't think anybody in the world completely understands it. I discussed it with Brother Kenneth Hagin, and he doesn't. Neither do I. The only thing I can tell you is that there's a gift called the gifts of healings in 1 Corinthians, chapter 12, and it's available for the Church.

But God only gives His healing power out where healing scriptures are taught. God only gives His healing power out where somebody is bold enough and honest enough to stand up for God and say, ''Jesus is your healer, and He wants to heal you right now.''

You've got to tell them. People only believe what they've been taught.

I prayed three days one time, trying to get God to tell me why my mother died with cancer at the age of 37. On the third day of praying, the Word of the Lord came unto me saying, "I didn't kill your mother with cancer, son. I didn't have anything to do with it. I couldn't give your mother cancer anyway, because I live in heaven and there are no cancers in heaven."

"Jesus," I said, "she was a good Christian. She loved You; she was Your child. Why did she die at 37 years of age?"

I don't want to make you mad, but Jesus said, "Where she went to church, nobody ever taught her how to be healed. Nobody ever taught her how to receive My divine healing that flows down from heaven to the believer. She's in heaven now, but nobody taught her how to be healed."

You better make sure that the church you go to is one that Jesus built. Jesus said, "The church that I build, the gates of hell shall not prevail against it" (Matt. 16:18).

The work of hell isn't even supposed to work in the church that Jesus builds. *It's supposed to be thrown out* by the leaders of the church. There's supposed to be enough of God's Word going forth to demolish anything the Devil tries to do to a church member.

Now, you may have thought that relative of yours who died young with a disease, died because it was time. The Lord came and got him and took him home. Is that what you thought?

Almost everybody thinks that unless they've studied the Bible. They have Christian relatives, and they just don't know and won't accept it as being the work of hell. So, they just think that it's God's time.

Always remember as long as you live: God does what you do. God's power is available for everybody.

If you have a short leg, God's power is available to make it long. If you need something new in your body, God's power is available to give it to you. If you've got a disease in your body that you've had for a long time, there's no reason for it to stay any longer. The power of God is available for you, if I can talk you into believing it.

Let's read verses 1 through 9 of the twelfth chapter of First Corinthians again.

> Now concerning spiritual gifts, brethren, I would not have you ignorant.
>
> Ye know that ye were Gentiles, carried away unto these dumb idols, even as ye were led.
>
> Wherefore I give you to understand, that no man speaking by the Spirit of God calleth Jesus accursed: and that no man can say that Jesus is Lord, but by the Holy Ghost.
>
> Now there are diversities of gifts, but the same Spirit.
>
> And there are differences of administrations, but the same Lord.
>
> And there are diversities of operations, but it is the same God which worketh all in all.
>
> But the manifestation of the Spirit is given to every man to profit withal.
>
> For to one is given by the Spirit the word of wisdom; to another the word of knowledge by the same Spirit;
>
> To another faith by the same Spirit; to another the gifts of healing by the same Spirit.

I want to point out something right here. I was raised in a denomination that never taught me about God's healing power. That's the reason I didn't know anything about it. I hadn't been taught that God's healing power was a free gift to everybody.

We had our own slant, our own version of it. We believed that Jesus *could* heal people if He wanted to, or if He chose to. But we believed that it *might* be God's will to heal somebody and it *might not* be God's will to heal somebody else. That's not scriptural.

Let's look at verses 1 through 12 and 18 through 21 again.

To another the working of miracles; to another prophecy; to another discerning of spirits; to another divers kinds of tongues; to another the interpretation of tongues;

But all these worketh that one and the selfsame Spirit, dividing to every man severally as he will.

For as the body is one, and hath many members, and all the members of that one body, being many, are one body: so also is Christ...

But now hath God set the members every one of them in the body, as it hath pleased him.

And if they were all one member, where were the body?

But now are they many members, yet but one body.

And the eye cannot say unto the hand, I have no need of thee: nor again the head to the feet, I have no need of you.

If you're reading this and you're real healthy, not even one small thing wrong with any member of your body, you might say, ''I'm healed. I really don't need this.''

Listen to me, if you'll learn this now and get it into your spirit now, *when* the Devil comes to your body, *you can throw him out.*

So learn right now, while you're healthy and strong.

Smith Wigglesworth, in his writings, says that if you're going to wait until you get flat on your back with a disease before you try to believe in God's healing power and accept your healing by faith, you've waited too long.

You can't even believe it now. You want to, but you're flat on your back. You can't because you're having to fight that affliction and fight that pain and fight that disease 24 hours a day. The symptoms are so strong in your body sometimes, you're trying to give them attention, and you don't give enough attention to God's Word. You haven't taken the time to memorize those healing scriptures. You haven't taken the time to put them down in your spirit. They are not a part of you.

Remember: the only scripture that ever works for you is the scripture that becomes a part of you — like your right arm. It has to be attached to you. It has to be so embedded in you that it can't come out of you.

You may say, "I don't have God's healing scriptures in me that strong."

Then hunt some up in the Bible and quote them about a thousand times. Go around for about a month saying, "Jesus is my healer." *But do it while you're strong and well, sharp and healthy.*

Then when the Devil comes, you'll look at him and say, "Jesus is my healer," because you've got it in your spirit so strong. It just comes out of you. You have something to fight the Devil with.

But as long as you take the Bible and just nonchalantly try to believe it, doing what you want to, you'll be robbed of God's healing power. And you won't get healed either. You'll have to put up with it and spend all your money on hospitals and doctors.

Jesus Ministered Healing

I want to show you two of the different ways that the Lord healed people when He was here on earth.

If you're a good student of the Scriptures, you'll find out that Jesus had all the gifts of healings operating through Him. Jesus had healing power working through Him to heal *everybody.* He healed all kinds of diseases. (Matt. 8:16.)

Let's read in Matthew 17, beginning with verse 14:

> And when they were come to the multitude, there came to him a certain man, kneeling down to him, and saying,
>
> Lord, have mercy on my son: for he is lunatick, and sore vexed: for ofttimes he falleth into the fire, and oft into the water.
>
> And I brought him to thy disciples, and they could not cure him.

> **Then Jesus answered and said, O faithless and perverse generation, how long shall I be with you? how long shall I suffer you? bring him hither to me.**
>
> **And Jesus rebuked the devil; and he departed out of him: and the child was cured from that very hour.**
>
> **Then came the disciples to Jesus apart, and said, Why could not we cast him out?**
>
> **And Jesus said unto them, Because of your unbelief; for verily I say unto you, If ye have faith as a grain of mustard seed, ye shall say unto this mountain, Remove hence to yonder place; and it shall remove; and nothing shall be impossible unto you.**
>
> **Matthew 17:14-20**

Does Jesus say to His Church, to believers, "And nothing shall be impossible unto you?" Does Jesus say that, or doesn't He?

Of course, that case that you thought was impossible and all your friends thought was impossible — for that very reason: you get what you believe. And you don't believe victory unless you talk victory. Then victory comes.

Howbeit this kind goeth not out but by prayer and fasting (v. 21).

You might say, "I don't know why I couldn't make this disease leave." Or, "I don't know why I couldn't get this lunatic healed." Or, "I don't know why I couldn't get this person healed who the Devil was attacking."

You have to recognize if a disease has been caused by a devil, or by natural things, or by your ignorance or neglect (like getting wet and sitting in front of the air conditioner). It all depends on what caused it.

If it's the dumb Devil that has come and tried to possess you and take you over or oppress you, you need to deal with that spirit and cast it out.

Demons cause sicknesses, too. They'll come to kill you. *Always remember this: If it's a deadly disease, always take authority over the spirit of death.* Death is the enemy of

God. Take authority over it, break the power of the Devil, and claim God's healing power. Always do that when you're dealing with a devil of oppression or possession.

When you're dealing with a spirit that's a killer, you need to fast and pray some, so you'll have power over that thing and make it obey you. Some spirits just will not obey you unless you fast and pray.

If you think you can go along and just break the power of the Devil and get all kinds of diseases healed and all kinds of goofed up people restored back to normal, I've got news for you: you can't do it with some of them *unless you fast and pray.*

Jesus said right there, ''Howbeit this kind goeth not out but by prayer and fasting.'' It all depends on what *kind* you're dealing with.

If you're dealing with a normal disease, God's healing power can drive it out of you — literally, drive it out of you.

While I've been speaking on God's healing power, the gifts of healings have begun to manifest themselves, and devils have fits and everything else. Devils leave and the person gets completely healed. Devils leave and crooked legs straighten out.

When God's power starts dropping on the congregation, you'll find all different kinds of things happen.

But you can see that this boy that Jesus healed was put in that shape by the Devil. The Devil did it.

Let's look now in Luke, chapter 13:

> **And he was teaching in one of the synagogues on the sabbath. And behold, there was a woman which had a spirit of infirmity eighteen years, and was bowed together, and could in no wise lift up herself.**
>
> **verses 10,11**

She had a spirit of infirmity. Where does that come from? It comes from the Devil. That can cause diseases and afflictions upon you.

And when Jesus saw her, he called her to him, and said unto her, Woman, thou art loosed from thine infirmity. And (notice this now: a doctrine of the Church) **he laid his hands on her: and immediately she was made straight, and glorified God** (vv. 12,13).

They started making fun of Him for healing her. And Jesus said, **And ought not this woman, being a daughter of Abraham, whom Satan hath bound, lo, these eighteen years, be loosed from this bond on the sabbath day?** (v. 16).

Both of the conditions mentioned in this chapter were caused by the Devil. The woman got healed by the laying on of Jesus' hands. The boy that was lunatic got his healing because Jesus cast the devil out of him.

You see, God wants you healed. He always wills to heal you. And He has provided many different ways for you to get your healing. I just wanted to show you two of the ways that the Lord healed people.

Specialists

I've never known anybody that's been in the ministry since Jesus who when he left 5,000 sick people — some of them crippled, blind, demon possessed, and lunatic — everyone of them had been healed.

Almost every man that God gives His healing power to minister with, has one, and sometimes two or three things, that he can get nearly everybody with that particular disease healed. I mean, he just has absolutely wonderful results.

I know a fellow in my hometown that used to be a midget.

"What do you mean *used* to be a midget? You mean he's not a midget now?"

No, he's not. He's 6 feet 1 inch tall and weighs about 190 pounds.

I've known his family all my life. I went to school with his sisters. But Jimmy was a little boy that just stopped growing when he got to 12 years of age. Nobody could figure it out. The doctors couldn't figure it out. He just stopped growing. He weighed 92 pounds when he was 12 years old.

When he went to be examined for the army (of course they didn't take him), he still weighed 92 pounds. I think he was 4 feet 9 inches tall.

God called him to work with little children. He said, "God, I don't want to work with those little kids. I want to be big. Get yourself another man."

One day, when he was 26 years old, he was riding down the road. He was driving about 35 or 40 miles per hour. A drunk came driving down the highway doing about 95. They had a head-on collision. The boy that was the passenger was killed. Jimmy's legs were knocked out of their sockets, and his thigh bones, driven through his hips, were sticking out. He was crushed, but — for some unknown reason — he was still breathing.

They took him to the hospital. The hospital said they couldn't help him, but that they thought he would be dead in a few minutes anyway. They suggested that perhaps someone in Chattanooga could help him, but he'd probably die before he got there.

They took him to a big hospital in Chattanooga. The doctor there said, "There's no way we can help him. He won't live. There's no use in trying to operate on him. He's too crushed. Just put him in a room over there. He'll be dead by morning."

He had been unconscious. But he opened his eyes and said to Jesus, "Lord, don't make me meet You like this. I know You tried to get me to win souls for You, Jesus, but I never have won any. Jesus, if You'll heal me, I'll knock on doors for You. I'll win souls for You for the rest of my life, Jesus, if You'll heal me." Then he lost consciousness again.

To the doctor's amazement, Jimmy opened his eyes the next morning. He had lost about a gallon of blood. The doctor said, "I can't understand how this boy is still breathing. He even acts like he's alert this morning."

Do you know that Jesus makes blood? Do you believe that God's power can do anything? Do you believe that Jesus would have compassion on a little midget boy laying in the emergency room, crying out for mercy?

A few days later, there he was, still living. Six or seven days later they put 35-pound weights on his feet and started pulling his bones back through his hips. They kept him in the hospital for months.

One day when the doctor and nurse thought Jimmy was asleep, the doctor said, "You know it's a shame what's happened to this little fellow. He seems like a nice little fellow. But even if he lives through this, he'll never be able to walk again. Of course, I personally don't think he's going to live."

The Devil took that statement and bombarded his mind with it. "You'll never walk again. You'll be a cripple the rest of your life." And he became afraid that he'd never walk again.

Finally they sent him home. Reading the Bible one day, Jimmy saw that God has not given us a spirit of fear, but of power, and of love, and of a sound mind. (2 Tim. 1:7.) He started reading where Jesus heals people. He started believing that Jesus was his healer. He took authority over the spirit of fear and made it leave him.

The ambulance came and got him once a week for about nine months and took him to the hospital. Toward the end of the nine months, he found that in the Bible. In two weeks' time, after he broke the power of the Devil over himself, his legs and body began to grow. He got up and started walking around.

Every 30 days he'd look down and his pants were too short. He had to go and buy new trousers every 30 days, he grew so fast. He grew from about 4 feet 9 inches to about 6 feet 1 inch in ten months.

That's really the number one way to be healed: to find scriptures and just stand on them yourself. Just tell God that you believe it, and stand on it.

I believe God will do anything for you. I believe He loves you that much. All things are possible to him that believes.

The Lord has given Jimmy a ministry. I would say that 95 percent of the people who have bad backs that he lays hands on and prays for get their healing. God just gives them a brand new back. At least nine out of ten get their healing.

God does that sometimes. There are certain things that seem to work stronger through some people's ministry. God's healing power works through them and heals many people, but everybody who has a particular disease that they pray for gets healed.

I don't know, but it seems like if there is anything like that with me, it's bad hearts and crooked limbs. Sometimes people walk up to me in conventions with some of their limbs crooked. Sometimes I just start to pray for them, and they are made normal, right in front of my eyes. Don't ask me why it works that way with some people. I don't know why, but it does.

Sometimes God deals with me mightily at different places about people with bad hearts. He wants to give them new hearts — and He does.

He came on me strongly one time in Indiana at a convention. I was just sitting there, and my heart started hurting. I couldn't take it any longer. It felt like my heart was going to stop. I knew what it was. God had already shown me what it was.

The MC was going along, talking about different things. I mean, it wasn't important what he was saying. He could have said it the next day.

I was sitting there with my heart hurting so badly, I couldn't take it any longer. The Lord said, "Right now."

So I got up and called all the people with bad hearts down to the front. If I'm not mistaken, there were ten of them. They were standing there, and all of a sudden God's healing power just dropped on them. He just began to heal their hearts and give them new hearts. All of them fell over on the floor, right in front of the convention. Nobody even touched them.

The gifts of healings work differently, but they're still all God's healing power.

Jesus Confirms the Word

The Bible says that the Lord confirms the Word with signs following. (Mark 16:20.) He confirms the *Word*. The gifts of healings as listed in 1 Corinthians 12 are given out as the Spirit wills.

Always keep this in mind: the Spirit of God always wills to heal you. He doesn't always will to manifest Himself in the gifts of healings (drop it on somebody and heal him out there by himself). But He always wills to heal you.

The gifts of healings, given out as the Spirit wills, manifest a lot of times when I'm teaching the Bible. Now it doesn't happen real often, but over a number of years it has happened a lot of times.

I was teaching one night in a church in Baton Rouge, Louisiana. It was a missionary church with a couple of thousand people there. I was teaching, when all of a sudden, four or five people just stood up in the back of the congregation.

They said, "Brother Norvel, there's a crippled girl that has been healed here."

I saw a little girl standing up. The Spirit of God was all over her. I said, "Come down here."

When I said that, she just walked out and walked down there. I had no idea that she had come on crutches. I didn't know her high school brother helped her get in there. I didn't know anything about it at all. Nobody had prayed for her.

She came walking down the aisle crying and trembling, and a boy (he looked like he was about 16 or 17 years of age) was walking beside her looking at her legs.

He said, "This is my crippled sister. I helped her get in here. I helped her get out of the car. Folks, I'm telling you, this is my crippled sister. I helped her get in here." He was so astonished at his sister's legs being stretched out.

I said, "Come up here, honey. Just tell the congregation what Jesus did for you. What happened to you?"

"I don't know," she said. "I was crippled when I came in here. This is my brother, and he helps me get out of the car and in places. I was just sitting there and all of a sudden my legs began to turn warm. Then, it wasn't very long until they began to turn hot. When that happened, I felt strength come into my legs. Then, I just stood up."

Everybody around in the church knew that girl was crippled. They'd known her for a long time. And all of a sudden, she was standing there, tears flowing out of her eyes. It kind of shakes people up.

With my own eyes, I saw a supernatural healing happen when I laid my hands on a person in an Assembly of God church in Mississippi. I was praying for sick people on Sunday night after I had taught on healing.

I came to a man, and he said so simply, "Mr. Hayes, skin cancer is all over my body. I want Jesus to heal me."

I just reached out and said, "I curse this cancer in Jesus' name. And I want to thank You, Jesus, for giving him new skin." I'm sure I didn't pray for him over 30 seconds.

Then I went on to the next person. He turned around and was going to sit back down on the front bench there. He just said, "Thank you." He didn't notice anything. But when he started to sit down, he saw new skin was on him, and he jumped up.

He said, "Everything's disappeared. I've got new skin on me. People, new skin has come upon me."

People started breaking down, crying. It was the most simple thing you've ever seen in your life. The Lord put new skin on him.

When God's healing power falls on the congregation many times and starts to heal the people, that's the gifts of healings.

One time I was teaching at a university and it happened. I was just teaching the Bible, minding my own business. All of a sudden, some woman jumped up and shouted, "It happened right there! It happened right there!"

I looked back, and this real fancy, socialite-type woman was standing back there looking at her chair.

I said, "Lady, what happened right there?"

"I've been deaf for 30 years," she said. "And when you were teaching the Bible, you pointed here to where we were sitting. You said real strong, 'God will do anything for you if you'll believe Him.' And all of a sudden, when you said that, my ears went *bloop*. I started hearing everything, and it happened right there."

One time I was teaching at the University of Florida. One night I started praying for the sick, and God's healing power was flowing strongly.

A professor was there. He came up, and God healed him right in front of the congregation. His daughter was visiting from New York. He said, "My daughter's got a disease, and she's here. Would you be willing to pray for her?"

"Oh, sure," I said.

When she came up, God laid her out on the floor and healed her. The professor and his daughter both were healed completely.

The girl went back to New York and told a bunch of people in Kingston, New York, "I met this fellow, and God heals people when he prays for them. The Lord healed my daddy, a professor at the University of Florida, and He healed me. Tell some of the pastors. Write him a letter and ask him to come up here to Kingston."

They wrote me a letter and the Spirit of God dealt with me to go up there, so I went.

The ministers in that city had a meeting once a week. They would get together and have breakfast and pray together. The Lutheran minister told me that he agreed to let them use his church. It was one of those beautiful, fancy churches. It had real dark wine-colored carpet. There were two pulpits. One was way up in the air. You had to climb steps around in the back to get to it.

I sat there wondering, "Do I have enough nerve to climb those stairs?" Right before they introduced me, I decided I had enough nerve. (I'd always wanted to do that anyway.)

I spoke, and the first night 26 people came forward to get saved. I gave just a plain salvation invitation, and they jumped up out of their seats and rushed down front to get saved.

Then, when I gave an invitation for healing, there must have been 40 people who came forward. They were standing at the altar. All of a sudden a boy, about 22 or 23 years of age, who was supporting himself with two crutches lifted both arms and his crutches fell. He turned and walked right down the middle of the church. He went past a blind boy, and the boy's eyes popped open.

Thank You, Jesus, for the gifts of healings.

The gifts of healings are God's healing power flowing down through your body to drive out afflictions in Jesus' name. And they come as the Spirit wills. Of course, when you teach on this gift, the Spirit always wills to manifest Himself in the gifts of healings.

Prayer

You can accept your healing right now, on your own. You see, you can accept it from God's Word. That's the reason I pointed out several ways for you to be healed.

Say: *"Right now, I receive God's healing power to do His work in me, in Jesus' name. I receive God's love in me to do His work for me that I need right now. I command my mind not to be confused. I claim the peace of God.*

"I say my body is strong and not weak. I say my spirit is receptive to God's Word and God's power. I'm God's man. I claim God's best through the power of the ministry gifts of the Holy Spirit.

"Thank You, Jesus, for First Corinthians chapter 12. Thank You, Jesus, for the gifts of healings. They are a gift to the Church.

I'm a part of the Church. I have a right to this gift. I receive it, in Jesus' name.

"Thank You, Jesus. I worship You, Jesus. I praise You, Jesus."

6

The Gift of
Working of Miracles

I've visited all kinds of churches across the country and, as a whole, the Church knows less about the gift of the working of miracles than any other gift of the Holy Spirit.

God has a gift that is given to the Church called the working of miracles.

What is working of miracles? It's a power gift, where power from God is sent from heaven to earth to do something that's beyond the natural thinking of man. When God performs a miracle, a *supernatural* miracle, it's so hard for a human being to *believe* it.

But I've got *news* for you, my brothers and sisters: When God says He has a gift for the Church called the working of miracles, He means *working of miracles.*

He'll work a miracle for you any way you need it, not just in the healing line. He'll work a miracle for you on Tuesday afternoon while you're downtown if you'll believe that. God's power will perform a miracle when it's impossible to do it. That kind of power is available for the believer. But you have to believe it.

Getting God's Power to Work for You

How can you get it to work for you? First you must believe that *Jesus* is a miracle worker, and you must *believe* He is a miracle worker for *you.* If you don't *believe* that, it won't work for you.

Now pay close attention. Unless you believe, recognize, and are willing to confess that Jesus is your Healer, you'll never be healed. You may get a touch of God's healing power through somebody else, but it won't last. Unless you're a person who will tell people that Jesus is your Healer, and not be ashamed of it, that same affliction will come back on you. Lazy people never stay healed, never. You overcome by the blood of the Lamb and by the word of your testimony. Not the word of somebody else's testimony — yours!

If the Lord Jesus Christ heals you only one time by His mighty power, He expects you to tell people about that healing for the rest of your life. You may tell it so many times that you get sick and tired of telling it. The members of your church might get tired of hearing it all the time, too. Do you remember somebody at your church who tells the same thing over and over again? When someone testifies the tenth time you kind of nonchalantly go, "I've heard that same story over and over again for ten years."

Change your attitude! The first time you heard it you probably liked it. By the tenth time you ought to be shouting and rejoicing, not making fun of what God has done!

The working of a miracle by God's power is an explosion of power from heaven to perform a miracle from God that is impossible for man to do. If you want to know the truth, it's impossible for the mind to understand a miracle.

The only reason a person ever gets confused where God is concerned is that he's trying to figure everything out. *I've got news for you:* you can't figure everything out!

Can you go out into your yard where the flowers are blooming and figure out how that flower blooms? No, you can't. In fact, you can't figure out very much about God. Just believe it, that's all. I mean *believe* it!

The gift of working of miracles is all by itself, my brothers and sisters. The gifts of healing and the gift of working of miracles are two of the power gifts. They work closely together many times when God's power comes into manifestation, but both of them are completely separate and have their own unique way of coming into existence.

Because the gift of working of miracles is a gift of power, it can create things for you. God's power can be released to do what your human mind can never understand. Don't try to figure it out. You'll only wind up confused.

When You Believe in Miracles, You'll Enjoy the Results

One time God sent me to Southern Illinois University. They gave me a classroom, and I taught the Bible. While I was there, a psychiatrist came to hear me teach, then he asked for an appointment to counsel with me for an hour after the service.

He said, "I'd like to talk with you. I always take patients, but I'll be your patient this time."

When we got together, he said, "Some of my patients have been coming over to the classroom at the University Building to hear you teach the Bible this week. They've been coming into my office and begging me to come hear you. I told them I didn't want to come, that I didn't have time. But they just kept on and on. They had such enthusiasm about it, so I had to come this morning."

He said, "I must say, I've met a lot of people in my day, but I've never heard anybody talk like you. You sure do talk like you know what you're talking about."

I said, "If I didn't, I wouldn't be talking that way."

"Mr. Hayes, I guess you know that my mind is playing tricks on me. My mind is telling me that all this stuff isn't true and can't happen that way."

105

"Now listen, Doctor. God made you, and there's no use in you trying to understand everything about Him. Just reach in there and get all of the intellectual knowledge and all of those college degrees you've got, and pull them out. Just listen to me for the next hour just like a little child."

He said, "Okay."

"Doctor, you spend your time teaching people how to live. Your problem is, you haven't learned how to live yourself. You've been leaving your office for years after counseling with people all day, teaching them how to live. Then you go to the country club, sit there and look at the bottom of that cocktail glass after listening to your buddies tell dirty jokes. After you've laughed at all their dirty jokes, you say to yourself, "Is this all life has to offer?' "

He said, "How did you know that? I've been thinking that for years."

I told him, "The Holy Ghost knows everything. Didn't you know that?"

After we talked for an hour, I said, "Tonight's the last night I'll be teaching at the university. Are you going to come?"

"Are you kidding?" He said, "I wouldn't miss it."

That night I taught a message called "God's Double Dose" about being baptized in the Holy Ghost and receiving power to heal your body. When I finished, I said, "Now I'm going to give a double invitation. All of you who want to be healed by God's power, get out of your seat and come down here."

That psychiatrist was the first one there.

Then I said, "Now all of you who want to receive more power in your life, come over here and stand, and you'll get baptized in the Holy Ghost."

A gospel service was new to this psychiatrist, and he didn't know how to act. While he was standing there, he asked real loud, "Can I leave this line and go over and get in the other one?"

Everybody laughed, and I said, "Just take it easy, Doctor. Take it easy. God's in no hurry. God never changes. Let me lay my hands on you first. Then you can receive your healing and come over here to receive power."

I laid my hands on him, praying for him in Jesus' name that God's healing power would come into him and bring a healing. Then I said, "Now that you're healed, go over there and get baptized in the Holy Ghost and get power."

In about ten minutes that psychiatrist was talking in tongues. He'd believe anything I'd tell him. If I told him the moon was going to be blue tomorrow, I think he'd have believed me. That's why I gave him such a good recipe to follow at first. It didn't take him very long to learn anything.

You see, I told him to get rid of all that intelligence he had and to be like a little child. I told him to let the Lord Jesus Christ teach him by His Word and lead him by His Spirit, and he obeyed that.

After a year had passed, I got to talk to him again.

He said, "Brother Norvel, after you left last year, I started holding a prayer meeting in my home. My wife and all of my children got saved. It wasn't long until we had so many people we couldn't get them all in our house. We lay hands on everybody that's sick. We cast out devils in Jesus' name, just like you do. I cast out devils all the time. I lay hands on people in my office and cast devils out of them."

I got a letter from him a while back, and he said, "If you hear of anybody that wants a Christian, Spirit-filled, praying-for-the-sick, casting-out-devils psychiatrist, let me know. My daughter gave her life to Jesus, and she's worse than I am. She just believes God for everything."

He said that she and her husband were out in a field and her child fell into a well. It was built up high, and there wasn't any way they could reach over and grab the child's hand. They were desperate. They looked for something to stand on, but there wasn't anything. So they just said, "God is our helper. God loves us and God is our helper. We look to God. Thank You, Lord."

They looked around again, and all of a sudden, there was a big rock, just high enough to stand on and reach down and get the child's hand and pull him out. The rock wasn't there before.

Do you believe that Jesus is the Son of God? *Then you're special to God.* You're a member of His Church. You have a right to anything that's in the Bible, and the gift of working of miracles is in the Bible!

Do you want Jesus to perform a miracle for you? Just say, "Jesus, I believe You're a miracle worker. I believe God's power is available to perform a miracle for me."

God doesn't work on maybe's. *God works for believers.*

At a time when things get desperate, you can't get shook up. You've got to stand with patience and steadfastness and say, "God is a miracle worker for me. If I need something, He'll give it to me."

You have to say that. *You* have to believe that. If you don't, you'll never see a miracle.

Now concerning spiritual gifts brethren, I would not have you ignorant.

1 Corinthians 12:1

Look at that, Church! *God doesn't bless ignorance!*

As long as you remain ignorant of the gift of working of miracles, you'll never have one.

Get it out of your mind that God won't perform a miracle for you because He will.

Before you die, you're going to need God to perform some miracles for you. But just because you *need* it doesn't mean you'll ever *get* it. Most Christians don't, you know. But God will perform it for you if you believe it.

Elisha's Faith

In the Old Testament, Elisha believed God for a miracle. He believed God would perform one for him:

> **And the sons of the prophets said unto Elisha, Behold now, the place where we dwell with thee is too strait for us. Let us go, we pray thee, unto Jordan, and take thence every man a beam, and let us make a place there, where we may dwell. And he answered, Go ye.**
>
> **And one said, Be content, I pray thee, and go with thy servants. And he answered, I will go. So he went with them. And when they came to Jordan, they cut down wood.**
>
> **But as one was felling a beam, the ax head fell into the water: and he cried, and said, Alas, master! for it was borrowed.**
>
> **And the man of God said, Where fell it? And he shewed him the place. And he cut down a stick, and cast it in thither, and the iron did swim.**
>
> **2 Kings 6:1-6**

Look what the man of God did.

If you're born again, you're a man of God. *You have the same right as any other man of God.* The Bible works for you. *God put things in the Bible for you to believe them for yourself.*

> **And the man of God said, Where fell it? And he shewed him the place.**
>
> **2 Kings 6:6**

Now by the mind of the Holy Spirit, Elisha cut a stick, threw it into the water, and the axhead floated to the top.

I can just see your mind turning. *"Everybody* knows iron doesn't float.''

But *some people* know God's power can reach down to the bottom of the Jordan River and make an axhead come to the top of the water and just float there.

If you're like most people, your mind is telling you right now, "I can't believe that."

I know your mind can't believe that. You don't believe the Bible with your mind.

The Bible says:

> But the natural man receiveth not the things of the Spirit of God: for they are foolishness unto him: neither can he know them...
>
> 1 Corinthians 2:14

Let me add something to that, *neither can he enjoy them.*

> ...and the iron did swim. Therefore, said he, Take it up to thee. And he put out his hand, and took it.
>
> 2 Kings 6:6,7

"Do you mean God just raised it up off the bottom and let it float where they could just reach out and get it?"

That's right! "Why?" They were building a house. They had only one ax. It fell in the water. *They were desperate.*

I want you to see that Elisha didn't get shook up. He had faith in the miracle-working power of God. He just cut a stick and threw it there in the water, and the axhead started swimming.

Your mind is asking, "Why did he cut a stick?" *I don't know.* Why did Jesus put the mud on the blind man's eyes and tell him to go wash it off? *I don't know.*

There's no use in you trying to figure it out! You can't understand why God does things. He just does them.

God has His own ways of doing things. He takes believers step by step. If you aren't willing to take the first step and do what He tells you, then you'll never enjoy the big things of God. You will never *enjoy* the victory, and you won't *see* many victories either, because *you're trying to figure God out in your mind.*

The natural man doesn't understand the things of God. When you're dealing with God, you're dealing with supernatural power. You're not dealing with the natural. You're dealing with God Almighty Himself.

Balaam's Figuring

Now let's look at a Bible example of a man who tried to figure things out for himself.

God came and tried to get Balaam to go with certain people. He didn't want to do it. Instead, he got up the next day, hopped on his donkey, and started down the road. *God told him what to do, but he decided to do his own thing.*

God sent an angel with a sword, and the angel stood in the middle of the road. Well, Balaam didn't see it. He was thinking in the natural, but the donkey he was riding saw the angel. So the donkey turned out of the road. A donkey's got more sense than to run into an angel with a sword. He started through a field.

Balaam started telling that dumb donkey to get back in the road, but it wouldn't do it. He started beating it. Three times he beat it while the angel was standing there. The donkey got three beatings because it wouldn't go against the angel of God.

In Numbers 22:28, you see the miracle God performed: **And the Lord opened the mouth of the ass, and she said unto Balaam, What have I done unto thee, that thou hast smitten me these three times?**

You might not believe that. Your mind probably wants to say, "That's pretty far out there, Norvel. I guess you want me to believe that a donkey started holding a conversation — saying words."

That's right. When an explosion of God's power comes in, God can have a donkey talk if He wants to. He doesn't have to ask you.

You say, "Well, I can't understand how a donkey could talk."

You don't have to understand it. Just believe it.

Now look at Balaam. He starts talking back to the donkey like it was an everyday thing.

> And Balaam said unto the ass, Because thou hast mocked me: I would there were a sword in mine hand, for now would I kill thee.
>
> Numbers 22:29

He was really mad!

> And the ass said unto Balaam, Am I not thine ass, upon which thou hast ridden ever since I was thine unto this day? was I ever wont to do so unto thee?.
>
> verse 30

He said, "No, you've been good to me."

> Then the Lord opened the eyes of Balaam, and he saw the angel of the Lord standing in the way, and his sword drawn in his hand: and he bowed down his head, and fell flat on his face. And the angel of the Lord said unto him, Wherefore hast thou smitten thine ass these three times? behold, I went out to withstand thee, because thy way is perverse before me.
>
> verses 31,32

Balaam was wrong before God. When you're not led by the Spirit of God, you start going down the wrong road. When you start doing your own thing, sometimes you get so far away from God that you grieve Him because you don't believe Him. But if you believe God, when you need it, a miracle is a free gift from Him.

God's power is your miracle worker. It's a free gift to you, and it can even create things that you need. It can take things away, make them disappear. You can look away from something, and it's gone.

Your natural mind can't understand that!

You're not supposed to try to understand with your natural mind anyway. Remember? The Bible says your natural mind can't understand the things of God.

You know, God has lots of compassion for human beings. Why? Because they're so dumb. Isn't the story of Balaam something? His donkey was more spiritual than he was.

I don't know if you know it yet or not, but where some things of God are concerned, we humans are pretty ignorant about what He wants to do for us.

All you have to do is follow His Spirit, do what He says do, and He'll perform a miracle for you.

The Orange Grove Miracle

I've got a little mission in Florida. God moved on me one morning and told me to buy a place on the side of a highway and make a mission out of it. It cost $90,000.

Close to our mission, there is one subdivision called Beverly Hills, where about 7,000 retired people live.

One time I was at the mission, and God showed me an orange grove with orange trees, laid out in rows on about 25 acres. God wanted me to buy it.

A couple of years ago, a big freeze came to Florida. My orange grove was covered with snow, icicles hanging from the trees, limbs hanging all the way to the ground, loaded with ripe oranges in January. My neighbor had a grove right across the street from me that was in the same condition.

If you know anything about citrus at all, you know that when this happens, you not only don't have any oranges, you don't have any trees. You might as well start knocking them down and planting a new grove.

In the natural my orange grove was dead, all the trees. But I believe the 12th chapter of 1 Corinthians. *I believe God's power will do anything for you if you can believe it.* So I just pulled my car up to my orange grove and sat there in the car by myself. I was afraid to take anybody with me because I was afraid they wouldn't believe it. When you want a miracle, you've got to get all unbelief away from you. So I went out by myself.

I sat there and looked at that orange grove, icicles hanging off the branches, knowing in the natural that every tree was dead, never to bear another orange.

I said, "Lord Jesus, I obeyed You early one morning when Your Spirit came upon me and told me to buy this property, start a mission, and work from door to door with these elderly people. I spent $90,000 buying this property, and I started a mission for You. And I thank You for every soul that's been saved.

"Now I believe You are a miracle worker and that Your power is available for me. I come to You, heavenly Father, in Jesus' name, and I bring this orange grove before You. I ask You to release Your miracle-working power from heaven and let it come and hover over every tree and protect it.

"And I say with my mouth that my trees will live and not die because Jesus said I can have whatever I say. I believe that Your power will protect my trees. Thank You, Lord."

When I got through, I watched over the next three or four days as the sun popped out. The ice began to melt, and every orange on my trees fell off. Every leaf on my trees fell off. The same thing happened to my neighbor's trees.

I kept saying, "Thank You, Lord, for protecting my trees by Your mighty power."

About three or four weeks later it was time for the trees to start budding. Buds began to come out on all of my trees. Not on one of them. Not on 95 percent of them. *I said on all of them!*

I sold 2,500 bushels of oranges!

My neighbor's trees had died, and every other tree around there had died — except mine!

I know God loves my neighbor, but my trees lived and his died. Why? Because I believed God for a miracle.

I was in my neighbor's office one day, and he said to me, "Mr. Hayes, you know it's amazing what happened. Your trees lived and mine died. Somebody told me you went up there in the snow and prayed. Is that true?"

I said, "Oh yeah. I went up there and prayed and asked God's power to come down over my trees and perform a miracle. God's got more power than a snowstorm and the Devil."

He said, "I want to know how to do that. Do you mind if I borrow your tapes?"

"No, go ahead. I don't mind. You just read the Bible, that's all. You believe God is a miracle worker. It's that simple."

You see, even the orange experts can't understand what happened.

But that's where God's power comes in. God releases an explosion of His power to give you a miracle if you need one, if you believe He's a miracle worker.

My Daughter's Hands

My daughter began to get knots all over her, especially on her hands. I couldn't do anything about it. I prayed and prayed. Then I got the surgeon to cut them off. But they came back and brought all their cousins and brothers with them. I prayed some more, and they got bigger. I prayed more, and they spread. I didn't know what to do.

I've got news for you: *Jesus knows what to do.*

I was walking through my living room one night, just minding my own business, and all of a sudden I went into another world. I wasn't in my living room anymore. I was in the world where God lives. He began to talk to me.

He said, "How long are you going to put up with those growths on your daughter's body?"

"How long am *I* going to put up with them? They're not on me, Jesus."

He said, "You're the head of this house."

Some men don't realize that what happens in their house is their fault — theirs and the Devil's. The Lord just plainly told me in no uncertain terms that it was my fault because my daughter had 42 knots on her body.

How could it be my fault? The Devil put them there. *I know, but I had the right, the authority, the power, and Jesus' name to break his power and throw him out, to claim a miracle from God for my daughter.* The sad part of it was, I hadn't done it. So as the days, weeks and months went on, her little body had become more and more covered with knots. Because of my ignorance of the gift of working of miracles and my failure to take authority over the Devil in my own house, my daughter had the ugliest hands in high school.

God told me to curse those things in His name, and they would disappear. But He told me I had to believe and not doubt.

The moment He said that, I began to come back into my body. Standing there in my living room, I was turning back into Norvel Hayes again. I found myself standing there weeping and shaking.

I was desperate. My daughter had been pleading with me to help her. Her hands were so ugly she was ashamed even to have a date.

When I got back from talking to God, I walked in and cursed them in Jesus' name, told them to die and disappear. I claimed the victory for God's power to come and give my daughter new hands, to perform a miracle for her.

You have to say what you mean. As long as you flim flam around and shrug off your responsibility of standing boldly on God's Word, I've got news for you: you aren't going to get a thing. All you're going to be doing is a bunch of praying.

You can be a Bible teacher, a Bible preacher, an evangelist, or anything you want, but if you don't stand on God's Word for your own house, the Devil will come in and smite your family. You have to throw the Devil out.

You have to get angry at the Devil and claim God's power by faith.

One afternoon, I heard a noise in Zona's room, like a dresser turning over. She came running down the hallway, holding her hands in front of her, crying, "Daddy! Daddy! This scares me. This is spooky. Look at my hands. *I've got new hands! I've got new hands!*"

I looked, and both of her hands were shiny. They were the most beautiful hands I've ever seen on a 16-year-old girl. I took her little hands and held them up. They looked like they had baby skin on them, so rosy and fresh looking, like a baby's skin after a bath.

She said, "I was just standing there, Daddy, and I looked off a few seconds. When I looked back, I had new hands! I have new hands! I can understand Jesus doing something for you because you work for Him, Daddy. Do you mean to tell me Jesus loves a 16-year-old girl enough to give her new hands?"

I walked over to her and took her hands again. I said, "Yes, honey, Jesus loves 16-year-old girls enough to come to their house and give them a complete miracle of brand new hands."

I want you to know that I testify about my daughter's hands all the time. I share it whenever I get a chance. I've shared it on TV several times, and when I shared it on TV in Los Angeles, the emcee started to cry so much he just couldn't do anything. Wherever I tell it, the Spirit of God just anoints and hovers over me as I tell of God's miracle for my daughter.

You see, God wants you to know and to believe that He is a miracle-working God.

I want you to know that you can come to the place where you believe the Bible for yourself. You can believe for your own miracles. When things look impossible, look to God and believe Him yourself. Just stand there because you're a child of God, saying, "I believe God," and He will release His power for you. It's an explosion of power that is great enough to cover orange trees. It's an explosion of power that can make an axhead float. It's enough power to make a donkey talk. It's enough power to create brand new hands. It's an explosion of power to give you whatever you want, and God does it so easy.

An explosion of power came to my house to give my daughter brand new hands. Every time I call her on the phone and say, "Well, honey, the Holy Ghost told me to tell them about the miracle Jesus did for your hands," she always asks, "Did you tell them, Daddy, that when Jesus gave me a miracle none of those knots ever came back?" Nothing ever came back. God is a miracle-working God.

A miracle is a gift. The gift of working of miracles is for you, as the Spirit wills. But pay attention. The Holy Spirit always wills for those people who believe the 12th chapter of 1 Corinthians. You see, that's the beautiful part. *The Spirit always wills for Bible believers!* Glory be to God forever.

A Prayer for Miracles

If you *need* a miracle from God, and you *want* a miracle from God, and you *believe* that Jesus is your miracle worker, *receive* your miracle now. It doesn't make any difference what it is. Jesus will give you the miracle you need. It is given by the Spirit of God, as the Spirit wills.

Say: *"Thank You, Jesus. You are a miracle worker. The Word is true. The truth shall bring me a miracle, if I believe it. And I believe it. It is a gift, free from heaven, to the believer. It is an amount of power that explodes and comes and does the impossible.*

"Thank You, Jesus, for the twelfth chapter of First Corinthians. I receive my miracle in Jesus' name. Thank You, Jesus, for my miracle."

7

The Gift of Prophecy

As we've seen, the nine *gifts of the Spirit* are recorded in the Bible by Paul, through the inspiration of the Holy Ghost. God gives these gifts to the *Body of Christ* and to individuals through the Holy Ghost living within them. And God does not want you to be ignorant of these gifts.

In this chapter, we are going to take a closer look at *the gift of prophecy*. You may say, "I don't necessarily need prophecy."

Yes you do. *The gift of prophecy* will change your whole life. It is so important that you know this. God had it recorded in the Bible, so you would not be ignorant of it.

Given by the Holy Ghost

You cannot prophesy just because you want to. There have been a lot of little home prayer meetings — where everybody in the house prophesies. One will say something, another person will say something, and so forth. That is not the *gift of prophecy*. I'm not saying that the words spoken are not from God. They may come from God. But that is not the *gift of prophecy* in operation.

The *gift of prophecy* is words of English given to an individual's spirit by the Holy Ghost — as the Spirit wills. These words begin to boil up out of that person's spirit, *supernaturally*. That is when *the gift of prophecy* comes into operation.

The gift of prophecy edifies or builds you up in God. It builds up the Church — in God. The *gift of prophecy* comes

121

as the Spirit wills. If it boils up inside you, and you refuse to give it out, that grieves the Lord. I have sometimes had God angry with me when I didn't want to prophesy. I have begged, "Please God; have mercy on me, Jesus." I have thought I was going to die. When God gives you something to prophesy, He gives it to you supernaturally, and He wants His Word spoken out.

The gift of prophecy brings great blessings to the whole Body of Christ.

Sometimes, the Holy Ghost will bring blessings to an entire congregation at one time. The beautiful thing about the *gift of prophecy* is it has its own unique way of working and bringing blessings from heaven to the people. It can bring blessings to any number of people at one time.

But the manifestation of the Spirit is given to every man to profit withal.

1 Corinthians 12:7

You will receive profit from the manifestation of the *gift of prophecy*.

If the *gift of prophecy* starts boiling up inside you in public assembly, it is necessary that you speak it out. But God may never call you to prophesy in public. It can be just for your own private prayer life. Prophecy can be used in your own family. But if *the gift of prophecy* operates in you, it is by the Holy Ghost Who lives within you.

The Lord once told me not to prophesy in churches unless I receive the pastor's permission. I am only telling you what He told me. But if you know that it is all right for you to prophesy, then go ahead. You don't have to worry about anything when it is of God. It will work out right. The peace of God will be there, and everybody will be built up.

Be Sure It Is of God

You should always be certain that the prophecy is of God, because there are familiar spirits that may want you to prophesy. Familiar spirits will come and imitate prophecy. You have to watch that. If you are just thinking something in your head, don't speak it out. If it *is* of God, just allow it to boil up out of you. It is then that it builds up the congregation, and it builds you up, too.

Again God wants the *Body of Christ* not to be ignorant of spiritual gifts: **Now concerning spiritual gifts, brethren, I would not have you ignorant** (1 Cor. 12:1).

If God uses you in the manifestation of the gifts of healing, or the gift of faith, or some of the power gifts, you will have a good walk with God. You will become a dedicated Christian. But you will never get to the point where you don't need *the gift of prophecy* in your life. You should hunger after *the gift of prophecy.* You should never get to the point that you don't want somebody who is of God to prophesy to you. God would not have you ignorant.

What Is Prophecy?

Prophecy is when God manifests Himself supernaturally to the spirit of man. He puts words into man's spirit in a known language. Prophecy is used by God to bring a great message.

Prophecy is not manifested in the same way as the *gift of tongues* and *interpretation.* If you are to prophesy, God gives words to you in a known language. It comes out of your spirit supernaturally, as it is given to you by the Spirit of God. When God chooses to use an individual, He releases His power into that person's spirit, and He creates words in a known language.

There is the office of a prophet, and there are those God chooses to prophesy at times.

Dr. Kenneth E. Hagin is a true prophet of God. He is divinely called of God to prophesy to the Body of Christ. If he doesn't do that, he is in trouble with God. He got into trouble with God once, because he refused to prophesy so much. Sometimes God will put several words in Brother Hagin's spirit. At other times He will only give him two or three words, and he has to step out on faith to receive the rest of the prophecy.

I am not called to prophesy like Brother Hagin. I am called to be a Bible teacher. Even though *the gift of prophecy* operates through me, I may go for a month and never prophesy. At other times, *the gift of prophecy* will come upon me and I will prophesy several times in one week.

The gift of prophecy comes to me in three ways.

1. God Himself will put words in my spirit supernaturally, and it will come out of my spirit like an explosion, full of power.

2. Like it sometimes happens to Brother Hagin, I will only receive two or three words, and I have to step out on faith.

3. Sometimes the Holy Ghost will use anointed songs or preaching of the gospel to give me a prophecy. I will be sitting there listening, then all of a sudden God will give me the whole prophecy, from beginning to end, supernaturally.

I have learned that when God does that it is always to build up the congregation. It is always given to complement the message. Usually the prophecy will contain the Scriptures that the person is speaking on or will complement them.

Sometimes I will begin to see a picture — like a mini-vision. The prophecy will begin to boil up out of my spirit, and I will speak out what I see in the picture. Nobody knows that I have seen anything except me.

Visions Are Scriptural

A vision is a scene or picture that God shows an individual by His Spirit that the individual has never seen before. The scenes are given to him (or her) supernaturally by the Spirit of God.

When this happens to me, two gifts of the Spirit are involved through the vision: *the word of knowledge* and *the gift of prophecy.*

The Gift of Prophecy in Operation

Several years ago I was sitting on the platform at a meeting in Indiana. I was getting ready to teach the Bible when I looked up and saw Brother Hagin and his wife walk in.

We went to the parsonage after the service. Brother Hagin was talking to the pastor, and I was talking to Oretha. I had no idea that anything was going to happen.

Mrs. Hagin said, ''You know, the Lord wants to use us, Brother Norvel, to bless a few young fellows and young women who have been called into the ministry. We feel like the Lord is going to give us a room that will hold twenty or thirty — never more than forty or fifty — chosen vessels that God has anointed to preach the gospel. God wants us to share our knowledge of Him and what we have learned over the years.''

Suddenly, as Mrs. Hagin was talking to me, I began to see something in my spirit: a campus — not just two or three buildings, but many buildings, on acres and acres of ground. The vision of that campus started boiling up out of me, and I just spoke it out right there.

That got Sister Hagin's attention! And it so blasted her, that when I finished she shook her head. She believed it, but she started to rebel against it. She said, ''Oh no! Oh no! No, Norvel. We don't want anything like that. We just want one little room somewhere.''

I said, "Oretha, it doesn't make any difference what you want. That's what you're going to get, anyway."

She said, "Oh no!"

I said, "Look for a campus. It's coming."

Of course, Brother Hagin had not even dreamed about *Rhema Bible Training Center,* much less believed he would be in charge of a campus. He thought that he was going to get one little room and train a few people who were anointed of God. But I saw *Rhema Bible Training Center* on the inside of me.

A few years later I was walking across the campus with Brother Hagin, and he said, "Well, Brother Norvel, see all this going up here. This is what you saw."

I said, "Not all of it! Brother Hagin, you are just getting started good." As Brother Hagin watches Rhema grow year by year, it shocks him. But it doesn't shock me. I saw it all before it ever happened — through the *gift of prophecy!* Now that prophecy has become reality!

The Importance of the Gift of Prophecy

In Old Testament times most prophecy was foretelling. Today, God not only uses prophecy to foretell, but to build up the Church. *The Body of Christ* longs to hear from God, and *the gift of prophecy* is the number one way that God talks to His Spirit-filled children. The *gift of prophecy* is given to build up *the Body of Christ* in God. It is for the edification of the Church. And the New Testament Church needs to be built up. That is why you need to go to church every time the doors are open.

How does *the gift of prophecy* work, and what is the importance of it? I will give you a personal example.

Several years ago I set up a meeting for Brother Hagin in Cleveland, Tennessee. At that time I owned six different restaurant businesses. Everything was going fine, and I was having no financial problems.

Brother Hagin was speaking one night, and I was sitting in the congregation, because I like to be fed when people like Brother Hagin come around. As he was speaking, he suddenly stopped teaching and began to prophesy. I don't remember everything that he said, but the church took it down, and it has come to pass already.

In the middle of the prophecy, Brother Hagin called my name. The moment he called my name, the Spirit of God hit me. It was like somebody just knocked me out of the world I was living in. I began to weep, and weep, and weep.

God said to me, *The enemy is going to attack your finances, and a dark cloud will come upon your finances. But if you will keep working for Me, and be faithful, and pray, and pray, and pray, and pray, you will come out of the attack. I will bring you out of the attack of the enemy, and you will be more financially successful than you have ever been.*

I said, ''Attack my finances? I don't have any financial problems.'' Along with the six restaurants, I owned a manufacturing company and a sales distributing company. I was making several thousand dollars a week, mostly from the distributing business.

About six months later the sky fell in on me. All of a sudden, three of my restaurants weren't making any money at all.

Then the Holy Ghost told me to check the books of my manufacturing company. I discovered that hundreds of orders were just sitting there. They were supposed to have been shipped out a month before. I checked on the bank deposits and learned that my secretary had stolen thousands of dollars. I could see that I was going to have to get some money to even get the orders out that were lying there.

Then I remembered what Brother Hagin had prophesied that the Devil was going to attack my finances and a dark cloud was going to come upon me. The Lord had said, *If you will pray, and pray and pray...you will come through it. And I will make you more successful than you have ever been.*

My lawyer suggested that I sell the corporation, so I sold the manufacturing company and got another factory in Memphis, Tennessee, to produce all of my business. I still owned my distributing company, and because I produced so much income through it, I couldn't give it up.

You may say, "Oh, it's a blessing to own a bunch of businesses."

It is a blessing to own businesses the way mine are now, but it wasn't a blessing then. It's not a blessing if you have to get money from somewhere else to even keep them open. That is a curse. You have never had a financial curse fall on you until you work all month and then have to borrow money to keep the business going.

This went on for about three years. I kept on praying, and praying, and praying. I kept my faith built up by praying. Finally, I asked my present secretary, "After you write your check this week, how much money do you have in the main account?" I really was ashamed to ask her.

She said, "Eighty-five dollars."

My main account should carry at least $10,000. It really should carry from $15,000 to $30,000 all the time. Eighty-five dollars was not enough to pay her next week's salary.

I said, "Mary Lou, I've got news for you! Look at that account. What does it say?"

"Eighty-five dollars."

I said, "I see thousands and thousands of dollars. Not three or four thousand, but thousands and thousands of dollars."

I walked the floor in my office and said, "Thank You, Jesus, for putting thousands and thousands of dollars in my account to pay all of my bills, with lots of money left over to spread the gospel and buy me what I want. Glory to God! Thank You, Jesus. And, Devil, I want you to know that I am going to keep on winning souls. I am going to pass out tracts on airplanes and wherever I go. Do you understand that, Satan? It makes no difference to me, I'm going to keep going on for God. I'm going to keep on being faithful in Jesus' name."

I kept on speaking and giving my testimony. They would introduce me by saying: "He owns six businesses...."

I would think, "If you only knew! I wish I was working at Westinghouse." However, I got up and gave my testimony and prayed for everybody. I would just walk around, like I had good sense, worshipping God and saying, "Thank You, Lord, for sending in thousands of dollars. I speak success over all of my businesses in Jesus' name."

I Did What God Told Me to Do

After I had been confessing prosperity for about one year, I grew very strong. I said, "Listen, Devil. I'm going to keep on going for Jesus and speaking for God. I'm going to keep doing what God wants me to do.

"Now listen to me, Satan. I will do it the rest of my life if all I ever eat are black-eyed peas and corn bread. You are a thief, and you have had it. If you think you are going to knock me out of the box by robbing me of a few thousand dollars, I've got news for you. I don't have dollar marks inside of me. I've got a vision of lost souls dying and going to hell, and I'm going to rescue all that I can. I will work for God if I have to preach or pass out tracts in the city dump. In fact, it makes no difference whether I speak or don't speak, Satan. I'm going to keep on working for God."

You ask, "How did you ever get out of it?"

I was in San Antonio three years later, holding some meetings. When I was getting ready to go back home, the Spirit of God suddenly fell on me. These words of prophecy began to boil up out of me: *Son, I want you to call Brother and Sister Goodwin, and call them now.*

The Goodwins were pastors in Pasadena, Texas, a suburb of Houston. I had not seen them for five years. In obedience to the Lord, I picked up the phone and called.

Brother Goodwin said, "Oh, Brother Norvel, we haven't seen you in so long. Please don't leave until you come to see us."

While I was there, the Holy Ghost started working. Sister Goodwin spoke in tongues to me, and Brother Goodwin gave the interpretation. God said, *If you will go to Tulsa, Oklahoma for Me, I will show you two things after you get there.* At that time I only knew three people in Tulsa. One of them was Kenneth Hagin.

At first I thought, "Tulsa, Oklahoma? What for?" Then I said, "All right, Lord, I'll do it."

I Passed the Test, and God Kept His Word

When God tells you something, it comes straight from heaven. It pays to listen to the Spirit of God, and to obey Him. On the way to Tulsa God moved on me supernaturally and showed me how to get my daughter saved. *And I would put that into action when I got home.*

I arrived in Tulsa and went to the Hagins' home. As we were visiting, the Lord said, "Go over and lay hands on Oretha. I want to bless her." As I reached out and touched her with the end of my fingers (as the Lord told me to do), Oretha fell flat onto the floor, crying and weeping. When Brother Hagin saw that, he dropped to his knees and began to pray in tongues. He did this for about an hour. After some time, the Lord told me that I could go home. Brother Hagin said, "Norvel, the Lord showed me why He sent you to Tulsa. He sent you here for two reasons: First, to pray for my wife and bring a blessing to her; and then, He told me to give you a prophecy."

The same man who had prophesied to me before about a dark cloud coming upon my business was going to be used of God to prophesy to me again.

God said, *You have passed My test of faith. You have obeyed Me, son. And because you have obeyed Me, My light is going to shine down from heaven. It is going to break through all the dark clouds and shine upon you. It is going to shine upon your finances. And it shall come, and come, and come, in abundance to you.*

I had not seen a financial blessing in three long years. But I had kept on walking steadfast working for God and praying, holding my faith up, going down to my office and walking back and forth across the floor saying, "Thank You, Lord. I see thousands of dollars in my bank account. Thank You, Jesus."

I owned a piece of property at that time, that I had bought several years before for $13,000. About ten days after I received that prophecy through Brother Hagin, I received a phone call from a man in Florida who wanted to buy it. I agreed to sell the property for $28,000. When I signed the papers, I had made $15,000!

Remember: I had not had even a $500 blessing in three years. But I refused to waver in the midst of the storm. All of my family had left me, and I sat in my house alone for three years. But I didn't waver. Don't let anybody talk you out of going to church, or getting involved with God, and His gifts of the Spirit. Don't let them talk you out of casting out devils, passing out tracts, or bringing sinners to church. If you will make up your mind to work for God, you will find that He has many ways to reach you.

Together with a friend, I had bought a piece of property for $15,000. While we were in Denver, Colorado, at a Full Gospel Businessmen's Fellowship International convention, we decided to have a prayer meeting. As we were praying, my friend came over to me and said, "Norvel, the Lord wants me to give you my part of that property we own together. Fix up the papers, and I will give it to you."

After he had signed the property over to me, I received a call from a person who offered me $87,500 for it. I said, "I believe I'll take it!"

I said, "Jesus, what am I going to do with all this money? One day I have $85 in my bank account, and now $100,000 is lying there!"

The Lord said, "You are going to spend it for Me. Or I am going to take it away from you."

I said, "I will, Lord. Just show me."

He said, "I will." He did, and I did! And the blessings began to flow.

Let me just pass this on to you. Prophecy, boiling up out of you supernaturally, will tell you where to go and what to do, when you don't know where to go or what to do.

I didn't know that I was supposed to call the Goodwins. How could I have known that? How was I supposed to know that God wanted me to go to Tulsa, Oklahoma, when I had my mind set on going home to Tennessee?

When prophecy comes to you from God, through somebody that knows God, and you respect them, it can bring great blessings — not only to you, but to many other people.

The gift of prophecy is important. God can give you something straight from heaven, as He did me, concerning my daughter. My daughter would come home from the Playmate Club at three or four o'clock in the morning, glassy eyed and on dope. I would say, "Zona, you came in at three o'clock in the morning. Honey, you know better than that. I didn't raise you that way, sweetheart. Don't you understand?''

God heard all that I was saying to her, and He told me that I hadn't been loving her as I was supposed to love her. He said: *I want you to tell her two things: tell her that you love her, and that I love her. Then I want you to shut up. When your daughter comes in, don't even ask where she has been. All that does is hurt the wound that is already there because you cannot help where she has been.*

I obeyed God; I didn't even ask her where she had been. I just told her that I loved her and that God loved her.

God sent an angel into her room and brought her back to Him. I was obeying prophecy, in my daughter's case.

God said, *Son, your spiritual pride is hurt. You are ashamed to have a daughter that goes to nightclubs and takes dope.* This is where it got me: He said, *I never turned against you when you were in sin. Why can't you love your own daughter while she is in darkness the way I loved you when you were in darkness? All of those sins you committed boiled up into heaven, in front of Me. How do you think I felt?*

I got away from that harsh, fatherly, protective type of love and went back to the way Jesus loved me. After I had done that for six months, my daughter said, ''Daddy, I am sick and tired of nightclubs. You love me so much, Daddy. And I know that God is in this house. I feel protected here: I feel secure here. You didn't raise a stupid child. I know that every friend that I have is a phony. And I am just as phony as they are. But I know God. I mean I have known God....''

God kept His Word concerning my daughter. Praise the Lord! Because I did what He told me to do.

When God Speaks — Listen!

The *Body of Christ*, as a whole, tends to take *the gift of prophecy* too lightly. When God speaks to you by His supernatural power through prophecy, you had better listen to what He is saying to you. He means what He says.

Sometimes, when *the gift of prophecy* boils up in you, it can be for your own benefit. However, nine times out of ten it is to bring a word directly from God for the benefit of the entire church body. He does this to build up the Church. He never drags His children down. That's why He says in His Word, **...let the weak say, I am strong** (Joel 3:10).

The fourteenth chapter of First Corinthians explains to the believer what God thinks about *the gift of prophecy* and what it does for you:

> **Follow after charity, and desire spiritual gifts, but rather that ye may prophesy. For he that speaketh in an unknown tongue speaketh not unto men, but unto God: for no man understandeth him; howbeit in the spirit he speaketh mysteries.**
>
> **But he that prophesieth speaketh unto men to edification, and exhortation, and comfort.**
>
> **He that speaketh in an unknown tongue edifieth himself; but he that prophesieth edifieth the church.**
>
> **I would that ye all spake with tongues, but rather that ye prophesied: for greater is he that prophesieth than he that speaketh with tongues, except he interpret, that the church may receive edifying.**
>
> **verses 1-5**

If you study the above Scripture, you will know that God considers *the gift of prophecy* of utmost importance to His children.

A Prophecy

The following is a prophecy that the Lord gave to the people when I was ending my teaching on *the gift of prophecy*. It is a perfect example of how He wants to build up His people.

...I will speak to you. I long to have you hear Me; to do just what I say. It will bring you blessings — blessings that I long for you to have. If only you will hearken unto My Word; every

time I speak. I have longed for a Church who would listen. I have longed just to speak to you, and have you hear.

Lift up your hands, and I will enter in; give Me all of you. Lift up your hands, and enter in to Me. Lift up your hands, and touch Me. Touch Me; lift up your heart; I'll meet your need. Lift up your hands, lift them up.

Oh, it is beginning. It is beginning to work. You think that it is over, but it is just beginning. I desire your minds to be transformed on Me. Lift your hands, and you will see. You see, My Spirit shall not leave you. See Me in all My glory.

You will see how I love you. How I love you! How I love you. I will make you into the one I want you to be, for Me. Take your rest. Take your rest in Me. Let Me do all I want to do. Learn to be just like Me.

Can't you see it is Me? Don't hold back. All that needs to go. Go to My love, and cling. Go to My love, and cling. How can it be so good? How can it be so good? Doesn't it feel good to be in My will?

8
The Gift of
Discerning of Spirits

Some people say, "I've got the gift of discernment from the Lord."

There's no such gift in the Bible as "the gift of discernment." There is a *gift of discerning of spirits.*

I am going to teach you on the discerning of spirits. God doesn't want you to be ignorant of the spirits around you — the spirits that you're in business with, the spirits that you live with.

God wants you to know the spirit and the motives of it. You can know it, too. The Holy Ghost will show it to you. The gift of the discerning of spirits will take you into the motives of the spirit and show you the depths of it.

Don't ever make up your mind about anything, to speak of, until you've prayed. Find out what kind of spirit you're dealing with. God will show you.

You can't *think* something is right. You have to *know.* You can't think with your head on the decisions you have to make in your life — who you will marry, or go into business with, or believe.

God doesn't want you to be ignorant of the discerning of spirits. He doesn't want you to be ignorant of knowing the spirit of somebody around you, if you're going to work with them, live with them, or have any dealings with them. God wants you to know their spirit. He doesn't want you to be ignorant of it, and you don't have to be.

137

The gift of discerning of spirits is given to you by God *"to profit with"* (1 Cor. 12:7.) If you'll listen to the Holy Ghost, you'll profit, too. He'll rescue you out of many pitfalls between now and the time you go to heaven.

You're just like me, my brother and sister, you're desperate for this gift. You have to have it working all the time.

Just as sure as you get to the point that you think you don't need it because you've arrived, the Devil will send deceiving spirits to appear to you and manifest themselves as angels of light. They are so strong that they'll make you think things are just fine when they're really all wrong.

I've got news for you. I don't care how smart you are, without the Holy Ghost, you're no match for the Devil.

But if you are open to and learn from the Holy Ghost, He'll give you the discerning of spirits. It will operate through you supernaturally. He'll speak to your spirit and let you know what kind of spirit you're dealing with. *The Devil doesn't put anything over on the Holy Ghost.*

You don't know about a person's spirit until God shows you. You might pick up a little. But if God doesn't want you involved with someone, the Holy Ghost will come upon you and grieve your spirit. He'll say, "No."

When the Holy Ghost says, "No," you'd better listen.

People think that because they know God they're going to get everything, but they're not.

You're not going to get everything just because you know God. *You have to know your enemy, too.* You have to know what God has given you by the Word. If you don't, the Devil will wring you out like a rag.

You have need of all nine gifts of the Spirit.

God said, "I've taken nine gifts of the Spirit and set them in the Body of Christ. I have them manifested as it pleases Me."

The gifts are all unique. They all have their own way and their own plan. They all have their own help for Christians.

You can't just enjoy seven of them. You need all nine. It is so important that you understand this. Each gift is different from the others. They all operate differently even though all of them are given out by the Holy Ghost. They all have their own place. One of them can't replace another one, even though two or three of them many times work closely together.

You need all nine gifts of the Spirit in your life.

To Know the Difference
Between Truth and Error

What is the purpose of the *discerning of spirits?* The purpose and meaning of this gift is to know and discern the spirit that motivates a person, whether truth or error.

God wants you to know the truth. That's the thing that sets you free from the Devil's power — the truth. The discerning of spirits will give you the truth about somebody else's spirit. Now, God doesn't show you everything about everybody's spirit. But He will show you the spirit of a person if He doesn't want you involved with that person.

God wants you to know the difference between truth and error.

> We are of God: he that knoweth God heareth us; he that is not of God heareth not us. Hereby know we the spirit of truth, and the spirit of error.
>
> 1 John 4:6

Because we are of God, we know the difference between the spirit of truth and the spirit of error. You better know the difference.

The gift of the discerning of spirits will show you the difference.

When you start knowing the difference between truth and error, you might as well get ready for the battle.

People tell me, ''I never had a battle in my life until I got baptized in the Holy Ghost. After I started praying a lot and taking authority over the Devil, I began having all kinds of battles in my life.''

You have to know God and you have to know the Devil. You have to know the plan of both and how they operate.

If you start for God, get ready to fight, because the Devil will try to stop you. He will do everything he can to stop you.

As long as you're not doing anything for God and you're ignorant, you're no threat to the Devil. The Devil is not going to bother you to any degree until he gets ready. He knows that you're ignorant and it doesn't make any difference anyway. You're not going to step out and do anything for God. He can pull all kinds of tricks on you and push you around the way he wants to. He can get you involved with all kinds of goofed-up people, and you don't know the difference.

God doesn't want you involved with goofed-up people. He only wants you to *witness* to them.

Paul Recognized a Deceiving Spirit

God doesn't want you to be deceived. When you listen to Him, God will take what the Devil does to you, turn it around, and use it for His glory. This is exactly what happened to Paul:

> And it came to pass, as we went to prayer, a certain damsel possessed with a spirit of divination met us, which brought her masters much gain by soothsaying: The same followed Paul and us, and cried, saying, These men are the servants of the most high God, which shew unto us the way of salvation.
>
> And this did she many days. But Paul, being grieved, turned and said to the spirit, I command thee in the name

> of Jesus Christ to come out of her. And he came out the same
> hour.
>
> Acts 16:16-18

Talk about a deceiving spirit! That wouldn't be an easy spirit to spot. You would never know without the discerning of spirits. You would never know unless the Holy Ghost showed you. It is so deceiving. See how easy you can be deceived? She spoke right words.

But the supernatural power of God that lives in your belly can show you a spirit — no matter what it says, what it does, or how it acts.

It doesn't make any difference what a human being says or does, that is no sign that it is a spirit of truth. I know spirits that talk about Jesus all the time, saying good things. They talk about God, about salvation, about men of God, and about the things of God. They may pray for the sick, but they're as phony as a $3 bill.

Let's look at verse 16 again. This is God talking. You need to know what kind of spirit she had. God explains it right here:

> And it came to pass, as we went to prayer, a certain
> damsel possessed with a spirit of divination met us, which
> brought her masters much gain by soothsaying.

She was a soothsayer. Now listen to that spirit:
> The same (spirit — not a different one) **followed Paul and
> us, and cried saying, These men are the servants of the most
> high God, which shew unto us the way of salvation.**

Brother, you have to have the discerning of spirits to know that spirit. That's enough to deceive anybody without the Holy Ghost. But the Holy Ghost has gifts and one is the gift of the discerning of spirits. When He manifests Himself, He shows you that spirit.

Not only does the discerning of spirits show you the spirit, it shows you the motives of it and the condition of it — whether it is truth or error. That's how important the gift of discerning of spirits is to you.

And this did she many days.

People ask me, "Why didn't Paul stop her?"

Paul was close to God. He wrote about two-thirds of the New Testament. Why didn't he stop her?

How could he stop her unless the Holy Ghost showed him her spirit?

What are you going to do with a young lady following you around saying good things about God and you? What are you going to do about it? What could Paul have done?

You say, "But he was Paul."

So he was Paul. He still had to have the gift of discerning of spirits in operation to show him somebody's spirit. Paul couldn't make God do things. He had to wait for the Spirit of God to manifest Himself.

Now notice this: **And this did she many days. But Paul, being grieved...**

That's God's number one way, in the ministry of discerning of spirits, to show you that you're dealing with a spirit of error — your spirit will become grieved.

Now you'd better do something about it, or run from it. I'm warning you. When the Holy Ghost begins to grieve your spirit about somebody else's spirit, you had better witness to them, get that spirit out of them, get them saved and baptized in the Holy Ghost — or get away from them completely.

But Paul, being grieved, turned and said to the spirit, I command thee in the name of Jesus Christ to come out of her. And he came out the same hour.

That happens many times. It didn't say he came out that minute. Sometimes when you're dealing with the Devil and evil spirits, they don't come out that minute.

I'm sure Paul just turned around and said, "In the name of Jesus Christ, I command you to come out of her," and just kept on walking. I feel sure in my spirit that Paul didn't even stop and pray for her. I feel sure that he just said it one time and just kept on going about his business. He broke the power of that spirit. The Bible says the spirit left her in that same hour.

I have broken the power of the Devil many times in people's lives and just gone about my business.

I've come to somebody in the prayer line and the Lord showed me an evil spirit was bothering them. I said, "I break your power, Satan, in Jesus' name, come out." Then I have just gone on and prayed for the other people. I've done it a lot of times.

Four or five minutes later, they fall on the floor in a fit. That spirit is wrestling with them. He doesn't want to leave. I'd be down at the other end of the line praying for some other people. The Holy Ghost would deliver them completely.

You see, I said, "In Jesus' name, you can't stay in this person. I'm not going to let you. I'm telling you to come out." That thing gets so mad because I did that. But it has to leave.

Jesus will confirm the gospel with signs following.

You can't just hang around somebody who is possessed with evil spirits and demand the manifestation right that moment. That's not the way you do it. You must have more faith than that.

That is *one* way you could possibly do it if you wanted to stay with them long enough. In certain cases sometimes you have to stay.

I did stay for eight hours with that boy I mentioned before who had lost his mind. The reason I stayed with him eight hours and prayed was because God moved upon me supernaturally and told me to go to a shopping center in Chattanooga, Tennessee. When I went there, a 19-year-old college boy had lost his mind. He was locked in a room with a guard. He didn't even know his own name. He had taken off all his clothes and gone out streaking. When he got out on the street, his mind snapped.

You have to watch that kind of thing. Maybe you don't know this, but what you do with your body affects your mind. That's why patients in the mental hospitals are all goofed up.

Mental hospitals in America are full and have a waiting list. Everyone in them could be healed, if somebody would recognize their spirit and what it's doing to them and give them the right recipes and correction.

Now, that boy I prayed with for eight hours got delivered. After eight hours of prayer, foam began to run out of his mouth and his mind snapped back into him.

He was from New Jersey and his daddy had been driving all night to pick him up. When his daddy came in, they wanted me to talk to him.

I said, "Mister, what kind of church do you go to?"

"I go to a Bible-believing church, Mr. Hayes."

I said, "All churches have the Bible, Mister. Do you go to a church where your pastor will invite people to come down who get confused and messed up and he lays his hand on them? Does he then claim the victory of God and command all foul, deceiving and confusing spirits to go in Jesus' name so that person can have victory and think straight? Does your pastor do that?"

"I don't think my pastor knows anything about that kind of stuff. I've never seen him do anything like that. What do you think I ought to do?"

"You ought to find yourself a new church and a new pastor. You might be a strong individual who could get along there with that kind of spirit. You might make it into heaven if they teach salvation. But your son doesn't have a strong spirit like yours. He has a weak spirit. He needs to be in a place where they have the ministry of the laying on of hands so God's clean holy power can go down through his mind and drive out every evil thought. Hands need to be laid on him every Sunday for the next three or four months just praying the blessings of God upon Him. Let some pastor who is filled with the Holy Ghost allow the Spirit of God to come through him and transfer into the boy.''

The Spirit Will Flow

Lester Sumrall taught me about the importance of spirits flowing, how certain people's spirit flowed. He didn't know he was teaching me. I didn't ask him to teach me. I got taught from him because of the condition of my own spirit.

I'd been going to his church and holding meetings for years. We even had a conference one time together. I might lay my hands on everybody during the week-long meeting.

I'd be in his office the day after the meeting was over and he'd say, ''Brother Norvel, wait right here. Let me get my three sons.''

He'd say to his three sons: ''Get in line here, boys. I want Brother Norvel to lay his hands on you one more time before he leaves.''

I'd think to myself, ''I've already prayed for them and laid my hands on them two or three times since I've been here this week. I wonder why he wants me to lay hands on them again before I leave.'' But I was ashamed to ask him. I didn't want to ask him.

On another trip back there he let it out. He said, ''Put your hands on them, Norvel, one more time before you leave. I want the spirit you've got to go into my sons. I like the spirit you've got, Norvel. I like the spirit that God has given you. I want it to go into my sons. I want all three of my sons to have it. Lay your hands on them so that spirit will go into them. It will be transferred from you into them. Claim them for God, Norvel, when you lay hands on them. Claim them for the gospel's sake.''

I would lay my hands on them and claim them for the gospel's sake.

None of them ever did go out and get a job in the world. They stayed right with God all the time. They never worked one day outside of the church. They have never worked one day for a salary or an hourly wage. They were trained and brought up right and have always worked in the work of the Lord — every one of them.

That's why I used to get people like Brother and Sister Hagin to come to my house and lay their hands on my daughter, Zona. I'd say to Sister Hagin, ''Oretha, take Zona in your arms. Just put your arms around her.''

Zona would always say, ''When Sister Hagin puts her arms around me and prays for me, I feel a clean, genuine, something real going into me. I feel it flowing from her to me, when she's holding me. She's so sweet. She's real. You know, I don't trust many women, but I trust her. Sister Hagin is real, Daddy.''

Brother, you know a spirit when you get around it. If it's real and straight from heaven, you know it. If you are sensitive to the Spirit and want to know the truth, God will let you know the truth. Remember what the Apostle John said? **We are of God** (1 John 4:6). We have a right to know the difference between the spirit of truth and the spirit of error.

It Makes the Devil Mad

God will show you a spirit that is not truth. The Devil doesn't want you to recognize him. It makes him mad and he'll attack you.

That's what happened to Paul. Did he ever get into trouble when he cast the Devil out of that woman?

> **And when her masters saw that the hope of their gains was gone, they caught Paul and Silas, and drew them into the marketplace unto the rulers, And brought them to the magistrates, saying, These men, being Jews, do exceedingly trouble our city.**
>
> Acts 16:19,20

You'd better believe it. You trouble the Devil too when you start discerning his spirits. The Devil doesn't want you to recognize him. That's one reason you're desperate, sometimes, to have the gift of discerning of spirits imparted to you. One thing that the Devil has in mind is for you not to recognize him.

He wants to work and you not recognize him.

I'm telling you, as you start taking authority over the Devil, it makes him mad. Absolutely makes him mad!

Watch what happened:

> **And teach customs, which are not lawful for us to receive, neither to observe, being Romans. And the multitude rose up together against them: and the magistrates rent off their clothes, and commanded to beat them.**
>
> Acts 16:21,22

You mean, men of God get beaten because the discerning of spirits operates through them? You recognize the Devil. You recognize error. You recognize the spirit that is wrong. The Devil doesn't want you to recognize him. (And you won't recognize a lot of them without the gift of discerning of spirits.)

> **And when they had laid many stripes upon them, they cast them into prison, charging the jailor to keep them safely: Who, having received such a charge, thrust them into the inner prison, and made their feet fast in the stocks. And at midnight Paul and Silas prayed, and sang praises unto God: and the prisoners heard them.**
>
> verses 23-25

Because of the gift of discerning of spirits, they are in jail with stocks around them, stripes on their backs, blood running down their backs.

You might say, "I don't think I want this gift."

And suddenly there was a great earthquake, so that the foundations of the prison were shaken: and immediately all the doors were opened, and every one's bands were loosed.

And the keeper of the prison awaking out of his sleep, and seeing the prison doors open, he drew out his sword, and would have killed himself, supposing that the prisoners had been fled.

But Paul cried with a loud voice, saying, Do thyself no harm: for we are all here.

Then he called for a light, and sprang in, and came trembling, and fell down before Paul and Silas,

And brought them out, and said, Sirs, what must I do to be saved?

And they said, Believe on the Lord Jesus Christ, and thou shalt be saved, and thy house.

And they spake unto him the word of the Lord, and to all that were in his house.

And he took them the same hour of the night, and washed their stripes; and was baptized, he and all his, straightway.

And when he had brought them into his house, he set meat before them, and rejoiced, believing in God with all his house.

verses 26-34

Do you see the end results when you praise God?

To Reveal False Prophets

And when they had gone through the isle unto Paphos, they found a certain sorcerer, a false prophet, a Jew, whose name was Bar-jesus:

Which was with the deputy of the country, Sergius Paulus, a prudent man; who called for Barnabas and Saul, and desired to hear the word of God.

> But Elymas the sorcerer (for so is his name by interpretation) withstood them, seeking to turn away the deputy from the faith.
>
> Then Saul, (who also is called Paul,) filled with the Holy Ghost, set his eyes on him,
>
> And said, O full of all subtilty and all mischief, thou child of the devil, thou enemy of all righteousness, wilt thou not cease to pervert the right ways of the Lord?
>
> And now, behold, the hand of the Lord is upon thee, and thou shalt be blind, not seeing the sun for a season. And immediately there fell on him a mist and a darkness; and he went about seeking some to lead him by the hand.
>
> Then the deputy, when he saw what was done, believed, being astonished at the doctrine of the Lord.
>
> Acts 13:6-12

Paul had the discerning of spirits manifested to him by the Holy Ghost and he saw the man's spirit. Paul saw that he was a false prophet. That's the reason Paul talked to him like he did.

When the deputy saw what was done, he believed, being astonished at the doctrine of the Lord.

Don't Be an Ignorant Child

I was sitting on the platform at a convention in Denver, Colorado, when a man was introduced. I wasn't looking at him and didn't recognize his name. I'd never heard of him in my life.

He walked to the platform and started to speak. The moment I heard words coming from his mouth, the Holy Ghost jumped inside me. My spirit became grieved. The Spirit of God said to my spirit, "Phony."

There were fifty or sixty other people sitting on the platform. Why didn't God show them? They are Spirit-filled believers who love God. Why didn't God show the people that booked him?

God won't ever give you the discerning of spirits unless you're available. You have to be open to it. You have to know about the twelfth chapter of First Corinthians.

Finally, the people who were booking this fellow recognized what he was. Not only did they recognize what he was, they caught him.

My brother and sister, you must have a great respect for the Holy Ghost and the gifts of the Spirit. If you don't show respect for it, God won't give it to you. He'll just let you glide along and live a sort of normal Christian life, just being an *ignorant* child of God.

You see, you can be a child of God, a dedicated child of God, and *still be ignorant.* But I'm telling you, the gift of discerning of spirits is free.

The Holy Ghost that lives inside of you wants to show you the spirit of someone else that you *need* to know. Don't go around suspecting everybody. Let the Holy Ghost manifest Himself.

You might ask, "How am I going to know when the Holy Ghost manifests Himself?"

Your spirit will become grieved. That's God's number one way to show you somebody else's spirit: when you're around them, your spirit becomes grieved. You won't feel right about the person.

God doesn't want you to be tricked by any deceiving spirits.

Look at Peter and John.

> **But there was a certain man, called Simon, which beforetime in the same city used sorcery, and bewitched the people of Samaria, giving out that himself was some great one:**
>
> **To whom they all gave heed, from the least to the greatest, saying, This man is the great power of God.**
>
> **Acts 8:9,10**

150

Do you see that? "From the greatest to the least." And they believed that.

My brother and sister, make yourself available and believe the twelfth chapter of First Corinthians, and that kind of junk won't be pulled on you. But if you don't do it, if you don't know anything about the gift of the discerning of spirits, it can happen to you, too.

Now I don't want to judge a person. I don't try to judge a person. I don't try to judge every little move they make or every little word they say that's not right. I'm not talking about that. That's the gift of suspicion. I'm not talking about that.

I'm talking about when the Holy Ghost moves inside you and gives you the gift of the discerning of spirits and shows you another person's spirit.

I don't care what they say, what they do, or how they act. I don't care how much they smile or how nice they are. I don't care how many times they get on the floor and pray. If their spirit is phony, it's phony.

> And to him they had regard, because that of long time he had bewitched them with sorceries.
>
> But when they believed Philip preaching the things concerning the kingdom of God, and the name of Jesus Christ, they were baptized, both men and women.
>
> Then Simon himself believed also: and when he was baptized, he continued with Philip, and wondered, beholding the miracles and signs which were done.
>
> Now when the apostles which were at Jerusalem heard that Samaria had received the word of God, they sent unto them Peter and John:
>
> Who, when they were come down, prayed for them, that they might receive the Holy Ghost:
>
> (For as yet he was fallen upon none of them: only they were baptized in the name of the Lord Jesus.)
>
> Then laid they their hands on them, and they received the Holy Ghost.

And when Simon saw that through laying on of the apostles' hands the Holy Ghost was given, he offered them money.

Saying, Give me also this power, that on whomsoever I lay hands, he may receive the Holy Ghost.

But Peter said unto him (because the gift of discerning of spirits began operating through Peter), **Thy money perish with thee, because thou hast thought that the gift of God may be purchased with money.**

Thou hast neither part nor lot in this matter: for thy heart is not right in the sight of God.

Repent therefore of this thy wickedness, and pray God, if perhaps the thought of thine heart may be forgiven thee.

For I perceive that thou art in the gall of bitterness, and in the bond of iniquity.

Then answered Simon, and said, Pray ye to the Lord for me, that none of these things which ye have spoken come upon me.

Acts 8:11-24

You can't buy the Holy Ghost with money. You can't buy any part of the gospel with money.

I meet preachers all over the country who say, "Norvel, I could have all kinds of money in this church. There's a man in town that has a lot of money. He wants to be one of the deacons (or assistant pastor, or song leader, or whatever). But the Holy Ghost showed me his spirit is not right and I can't let him do it. He can come to church if he wants to, but I can't let him do it."

I'm telling you, the Lord will move upon you and give you the gift of discerning of spirits.

The discerning of spirits enables you to see what others can't see. It will guard you and rescue you, if you learn to make yourself available to the Holy Spirit.

152

Prayer

Do you want the Holy Ghost to give you the discerning of spirits?

Say: *"Thank You, Lord, for the twelfth chapter of First Corinthians. I am trusting the Holy Ghost to give me discerning of spirits every time the Devil tries to pull a trick on me, tries to deceive me, tries to appear to me as an angel of light trying to make me think something is right that is not right.*

"From this day forward, the Spirit of God will rise up in me and give unto me the gift of discerning of spirits when the Devil comes and tries to rob me of the blessings, peace, contentment, restfulness that my spirit has in God. He will rescue me, by the discerning of spirits, from getting involved with evil spirits and deceiving spirits. I'll keep the peace of God because the Holy Ghost will show me that spirit as the Spirit wills.

"Thank You, Jesus. I'm born again. I'm free from the Devil's power. Thank You, God, for the Holy Ghost."

9

Tongues and Interpretation of Tongues

Why Tongues?

In this chapter on *the gifts of the Spirit,* I would like to emphasize that *the gift of tongues* and *the interpretation of tongues* have their own unique place. Nothing can take their place in the gifts series or in the Body of Christ.

You may say, "Well, what about prophecy? In your book on *The Gift of Prophecy,* you said that *the gift of prophecy* is powerful."

Yes, *the gift of prophecy* is powerful, but it is a completely different gift in the nine gifts of the Spirit. The gift of prophecy is to be spoken out supernaturally — in English — to build up the Body of Christ, and to tell things.

The gift of tongues and *interpretation* can be equivalent to *the gift of prophecy* when they are used by the Holy Ghost for the same purpose. But they are different gifts that are given by the Spirit as He wills.

The *gift of tongues* and *interpretation* are the last of the three vocal gifts of the Spirit. If you have studied all of my books on *the gifts of the Spirit,* you now know that there are three groups of gifts:

1. Gifts of power: *faith, healing,* and *working of miracles.*

2. Gifts of revelation: *word of knowledge, word of wisdom,* and *discerning of spirits.*

3. Vocal gifts: *prophecy, tongues,* and *interpretation of tongues.*

I'm sorry to say this, but most churches built on this earth are ignorant of all *the gifts of the Spirit.* The very things that God says He would not have us ignorant of are the things that mankind is most ignorant of. The Church is especially ignorant of *the gift of tongues* and *the interpretation of tongues.*

If you do not believe in tongues, and interpretation, what is your excuse?

You may say, "Well, I can't help it because I was born into a family that doesn't believe in *the gifts of the Spirit.* My relatives don't believe in *tongues* and *interpretation.*"

I know that you can't help that, but you don't have to stay like your relatives. Why would you want to stay like them? You have a chance to be like Jesus. You have a chance to believe in *tongues* and *interpretation.* You can get your Bible and see what the Word of God says about these spiritual gifts. You can read 1 Corinthians 12:1 and know that God doesn't want you ignorant of the nine *gifts of the Spirit.* God said that if you don't believe in *the gifts of the Spirit* it is because you are a Gentile, carried away by your relatives to dumb services. The reason you haven't believed in *tongues* and *interpretation* is because you have been taught a bunch of dumb stuff.

You may say, "Well, it may not be God's will for me to speak in tongues."

The gifts of the Spirit are for you. They are for every man. Let's read the seventh verse of 1 Corinthians 12 again:

> **But the manifestation of the Spirit is given to every man to profit withal.**
>
> *That means you!*

You may say, "But I believe in the Holy Spirit."

I am not talking about the Holy Spirit. I am talking about the manifestation of the *nine gifts of the Spirit* that God has given to the Church. They are all free gifts — as the

Spirit wills; and, of course, He wills to give them to the people who believe in the Bible. Remember the twelfth chapter of First Corinthians, verses 11 and 12 say:

> But all these worketh that one and the selfsame Spirit, dividing to every man severally as he will. For as the body is one, and hath many members, and all the members of that one body, being many, are one body: so also is Christ.

Let's continue reading concerning the Body, in verses 18 through 21:

> But now hath God set the members every one of them in the body, as it hath pleased him. And if they were all one member, where were the body? But now are they many members, yet but one body. And the eye cannot say unto the hand, I have no need of thee: nor again the head to the feet, I have no need of you.

Just because you have experienced salvation, or have been healed by God's power, or have had great manifestations from God, God says, "You had better not say, 'I don't need to speak in tongues.' "

God says that you do need to speak in tongues. Read verse 21 again:

> And the eye cannot say unto the hand, I have no need of thee: nor again the head to the feet, I have no need of you.

You cannot say that and be in His will, because God is God, and He is the Head of the Church. God put those things in the Bible, and He says that He would not have you ignorant of them.

If you say that you don't need *the gifts of the Spirit,* that is what God calls "dumb idols; coming from a dumb human." And I don't mean intellectually. You may be a professor in a university, but that is no sign that you have any sense about speaking in tongues.

You may say, "What are *tongues* and *interpretation of tongues?*"

When God has a message for the Church, He manifests Himself in your belly first. I will say it this way: When the

Spirit of God manifests Himself down in your belly, and it gets over to your spirit, then He wants you to give out a message in tongues — *supernaturally. The gift of tongues* operates *supernaturally.* You have it down in your spirit, and you speak those words out *in tongues.*

Then when God shows another person *in English* what you spoke out *in tongues,* that is *the interpretation of tongues.*

Both *tongues* and *interpretation of tongues* operate supernaturally — *only as the Spirit wills.* You can't *make* God let you give out a message in tongues in a public assembly. Neither can you make Him give you the interpretation of a message in tongues that has been given. It is as the Holy Spirit wills. Both *the gift of tongues* and *the interpretation of tongues* operate by the supernatural power of God being manifested inside of you. They have their own unique way of being manifested.

The gift of tongues is big brother, and *the interpretation of tongues* is the little sister. A big brother can do much more than a little sister. But in the eyes of God the little five-year-old sister is just as important as the eighteen-year-old brother.

The gift of tongues does a whole lot of things for *the Body of Christ,* and for you personally. Although *the interpretation of tongues* is just as important, it doesn't do as many things. Like *the gift of tongues, the interpretation of tongues* is a gift of the Spirit. It does the telling forth.

Some Benefits of Tongues

There are many reasons why God included tongues in the nine *gifts of the Spirit.* In this chapter, we will take a closer look at some of the benefits of *tongues.*

Number one: You can worship God in the spirit. Man is a spirit and God is a Spirit. We read: **God is a Spirit: and they that worship him must worship him in spirit and in truth** (John 4:24).

Number two: You can talk directly to God. You can pray in the spirit; you can sing in the spirit; as I said in number one, you can worship God in the spirit. However, just worshipping God in the spirit is not the only purpose for tongues. One of the main purposes is so you can speak directly to God *through tongues,* or a heavenly language that is given to you by the Holy Spirit. The Word says: **For he that speaketh in an unknown tongue speaketh not unto men, but unto God...** (1 Cor. 14:2a).

Number three: You can speak mysteries unto God. Tongues gives you a more fluent vocabulary. In other words, you want to know what to say to God in a certain situation, but you don't have the vocabulary. You, as a normal human being, with your natural mind can't think of what you want to say, or how to say it. Tongues makes up for your inadequacy.

We read again: **For he that speaketh in an unknown tongue speaketh not unto men, but unto God: for no man understandeth him; howbeit in the spirit he speaketh mysteries** (1 Cor. 14:2). You don't understand the mysteries and the sounds coming out of your spirit that are put there by the Holy Ghost. Though they are mysteries to you, they are not mysteries to God. He knows exactly what you are saying.

Number four: Speaking in tongues helps your infirmities. We read in Romans 8:26: **Likewise the Spirit also helpeth our infirmities: for we know not what we should pray for as we ought: but the Spirit itself maketh intercession for us with groanings which cannot be uttered.**

My brother or sister, you are just like me: you don't know everything, and you don't know how to do everything. In the following example you can see that the Holy Spirit made intercession with groanings that could not be uttered.

Brother Kenneth E. Hagin was going to hold a meeting in Cleveland, Tennessee. Two or three days before the meeting started, he came to my house to rest and have fellowship. Sister Hagin had stayed with her mother in Texas and was planning to join us a few days later.

As Brother Hagin and I were visiting, Sister Hagin phoned. She said, "Norvel, a pastor friend of ours here has had a severe heart attack. They say there is no hope for him. He is in the ambulance right now, and they are taking him to the hospital. Is Kenneth there?" I handed the phone to Brother Hagin, and Oretha told him what she had just told me.

That night we learned something about praying and interceding that we had not known before. We did three things and the Holy Spirit gave us a real assurance about our actions.

Number one: We both fell to the floor and broke the power of the devil over that man's body, *in English.*

Number two: We agreed and asked the Lord to heal, *in English.*

Number three: We started praying *in tongues.* We prayed in tongues just as hard and fast as we could. After we had prayed a long, long time, the glory of the Lord came upon us.

It was then that Brother Hagin fell over on the couch and started *groaning in the spirit* before the Lord. Then God gave him the interpretation. Brother Hagin looked at me and said, "Brother Norvel, you know we got hold of something tonight that I never got hold of before in my life."

This comes straight from heaven and it is scriptural. You will remember the Scripture verse that says, "You have not because you ask not...." It was when Brother Hagin started groaning in the Spirit before the Lord that the glory of the Lord fell upon us. He told us that we had prayed correctly, and that the man would not die.

I want to know everything that I can from God. We as human beings mean well, and we love Him, but sometimes we can get all mixed up and do wrong things.

I don't know why man wants to fight God so much. But God knows why. He said, ''You know that you were Gentiles, carried away unto those dumb idols.'' God loves you so much that He doesn't want you having a bunch of dumb idols. He wants you to come to the place where you will just believe what His Word says.

Confess this: *Jesus, I love the Bible. I am a Word person. Teach me, Lord, by Thy Word.* The way you learn from God is through His Word.

The Spirit helps our infirmities. In the case of the pastor, first we broke the power of the Devil over his body *in English.* Second, we agreed *in English* and asked the Lord to heal him. Third, we started *praying in tongues* until we felt a release in our spirits, and the Holy Spirit interceded for us with groanings that could not be uttered.

Number four: Speaking in tongues helps you to magnify the Lord. You may ask, ''What do you mean that you are supposed to magnify God in tongues? Is that scriptural?''

Yes, it is scriptural. Read with me: **For they heard them speak with tongues, and magnify God...** (Acts 10:46). If you wish to magnify God, start speaking in tongues right now.

Number five: Speaking in tongues brings the wonderful works of God. **Cretes and Arabians, we do hear them speak in our tongues the wonderful works of God** (Acts 2:11).

You may ask, ''What kind of wonderful works?''

All kinds of them: healings and everything.

''Do you mean to tell me that if I just speak in tongues Jesus can heal somebody?''

That's right.

"Well, how would I know that He is healing somebody, by me just *speaking in tongues?*"

You wouldn't know. It is none of your business anyway. Just go ahead and speak in tongues. *The wonderful works of God come about by speaking in tongues.*

Distance Doesn't Stop the Wonderful Works of God

Acts 2:7 says: **And they were all amazed and marvelled, saying one to another, Behold, are not all these which speak Galilaeans?**

You may still be wondering if speaking in tongues brings about the wonderful works of God.

Yes. This happened to me some time ago. And it can happen to you if you are available to God. He can use you to be the one who speaks in tongues. And by doing that it can bring great blessings to many people.

You can speak in tongues for an hour for God when He tells you to be the one to speak in tongues. And by doing that there is no telling what kind of ministry will go forth, or what kind of blessings will fall on the human race in different parts of the world — *just by you speaking in tongues, that particular hour, because the Holy Ghost told you to do so.*

I was holding a meeting some years ago in Toronto, Canada. I had one of my college mission teams up there. There were seven young people in a motor home. We raised up teams in that particular church to knock on doors. Then I was going to take the team and go with them to do some mission work in Canada. We were driving during the day and working in the churches at night.

That night at the service there were probably from 25 to 35 people. When I had finished speaking, the Spirit of God said to me, "Walk and pray in the spirit."

I started walking behind the pulpit, praying in tongues. I just shut myself off from the service and continued walking, praying in tongues.

After I had prayed for a long time, God's power was suddenly upon me. Then a woman began to cry, and sob, and weep. I didn't know why.

The woman said, "Brother Norvel, you don't know anything about this, but my husband and I have a daughter who is in her twenties. She is a missionary overseas, working with a tribe of people, and she has picked up a rare disease. We have just received word that she is not going to live, and we have no way to get her back home."

The lady had learned the language of the people from her daughter, because the daughter had been a missionary over there for such a long time. The lady went on:

While you were speaking in tongues and walking behind the pulpit, you began to speak out the wonderful works of God and the healing power of God for my daughter in the same language of the tribe that she works with. When the note of victory came, God's healing power swept over there where she is, shot down through her body, and healed her. Glory be to God! Thank You, Jesus!

Now, I wish to point out. I didn't know the lady's daughter, and I didn't know the language of that tribe of people. But you see, I was willing to obey God. When I began to speak out in tongues, that mother recognized the language. She knew I was speaking out the healing power of God for her daughter in that tribal language.

It is no wonder that God said speaking in tongues is a mystery. It is no wonder that Acts 2:11 said, **Cretes and Arabians, we do hear them speak in our tongues the wonderful works of God.** On the day of Pentecost, the one hundred and twenty were speaking in tongues. But the Arabians listened to them and said, "We hear them speaking in our language. They are Galileans, and they don't know the Arabian language. But we hear them speaking in our language the wonderful works of God.''

The Holy Ghost can use you like that.

The Holy Ghost can have you — if you will pray in tongues — to speak out another language. You will not know what you are saying. But if you will obey God when He tells you to pray in tongues, He can let you speak out another language of a tribe of people, and He will start healing the people.

God knew that those parents were good Christian people who loved Him. He knew about their daughter who had been giving her life to those people. He knew that she was dying from a rare disease. And He used me to pray in tongues for her.

The Holy Ghost fell on that congregation, and fell on me, and gave us a note of victory. Jesus healed her. The daughter lived.

Confess this: *Thank You, Jesus, for tongues and for being able to pray in the spirit. Tongues are a mystery to me; but, Jesus, they are not a mystery to You. You are the Healer. You are the One Who does the wonderful works of God by Your Spirit. Thank You, Lord.*

When I was teaching on this subject, the following prophecy came forth through Reverend Buddy Harrison as he obeyed the Lord:

> For it is entering into that time and place that I will show My mercy. Yes, even My grace. And you will find yourself moving forth in power. Yes, it will cause the works of God to bring forth the healing power to move into that place.
>
> Do not hesitate; no, do not wait, or you will be too late. But enter in and say forth all that which the Spirit would bid you to say. For it will cause you to enter into a brand new day. And you will be able to walk forth in the land. And you'll be strong and cause others to stand.
>
> So be diligent to speak the wondrous works of God. For it is speaking the Word that causes it to work. So, rejoice and

know that as you speak it forth and believe it in your hearts, it shall surely come to pass.

For see, you are not aware of many times that you are standing in a place of prayer. Yes, even in the congregation, you are unaware. For your spirit does know because it is in harmony and fellowship with God. But the mind does not comprehend or enter therein.

And you will find yourself even in a place of worship in congregations throughout the land, that you will sit there, and you will be able to worship the Lord and speak in other tongues. And say, "Yes, oh, Lord, we do magnify You."

And you will find a refreshing, yes, it will be a blessing even unto you. For you will build yourself up. And you will find strength to rise within. And yes, it will cause you to be rejoicing and to be filled within.

And you will say, "Oh, bless the Lord, oh my soul, and all that is within me! It is well, for He hath accomplished all that thing, and He hath kept me from the pit of hell." And you will be able to magnify, and give thanks, glorious and well.

So that is proper. So continue on, and do that as well. But you will find yourself coming into a place in the many days ahead, and oh, don't think for a moment that it will be a thing that you will dread. But it will be a thing of the heart, where the Spirit will intercede. And, oh, that is the moment you too will meet the need.

And you will be able to enter in and say, "Oh, bless the Lord!" And the Spirit will sweep within. And you will cause your knee to bow, and there you will be able to enter therein. And you will stand in the gap. And you will take their place. And oh, it will be in that, that you will understand mercy and grace.

For you will bow down and you will declare, "Oh, my God! Oh, my soul! Oh, it doth travail. I need to be made whole." And you will see that there is in that place when you stand: fullness — fullness that should be brought to others in the land.

And oh, there will be as though you are dead in weight. And oh, it seemed that the enemy hath come, and that the Lord is too late. There will be crying, and moaning, and agony there. And you'll say, "Oh, my soul is full of despair!" And oh, it will be heavy, but as you continue on groaning there. For you see, that is where the Spirit is — He lies deep within.

And He will give forth into victory in that hour. And you'll come to that place! Oh, the victory — it shall shout in the air. And you'll catch yourself: "Ah-ha! It's done!" For that which you have spoken has been won.

You see, you declared it, because you believed it in your heart. And you said, "Oh, thanks be unto God! It is not dead. But I am alive through Jesus, my Lord! And I'm well! Oh, thanks be unto God! He hath delivered my soul from hell. Ha-ha-ha! Oh, glory to the Lamb! Oh-ho, hallelujah! I sing it in the land!"

And there will be rejoicing. Ah-ha! There's victory everywhere. You see, you stood in the gap. And oh, it will not go any further than the enemy will be. You see, you have conquered him: you are what Christ has made thee.

Say with me: *Oh, thanks be unto God for His wonderful works that know no distance.*

Do Not Neglect Praying in Tongues

Christians should thank God for *the gift of tongues* and *the gift of interpretation of tongues.* God has given them the nine *gifts of the Spirit* for their benefit. Christians need to speak in *tongues* — magnifying and glorifying God Almighty and His works.

Reader, you get into trouble when you forget *tongues,* because you leave the gate wide open for the Devil to come in.

During many meetings that I have held in large churches or state conventions, the Holy Ghost has dealt with me, saying, "Oh, son, out there in the congregation many of My children are cold and indifferent. I have saved them, and they love Me, basically. I baptized them in the Holy Ghost not ten, fifteen, twenty, or thirty years ago. And they have not prayed in tongues for a month. Some of them have not prayed in tongues in six months. Some have not prayed in tongues for a year. It was new and refreshing and glorious when they received it, but now it is like an everyday thing. It is like a meal to them.''

Some Christians say, ''Praying in tongues is like another meal to me. I eat three meals a day, and so what? Another meal. I can take a drink of water now, or I can wait an hour from now.''

That is sad. I belong to God, and He will deal with me about giving an invitation for Christians — Christians who have been baptized in the Holy Ghost, but they have not prayed in tongues for a week, or perhaps a month. It has gotten to be just an old thing to them.

Understand this: Don't ever let praying in tongues get to be an old thing to you. If you do, *this is when you fall off the cliff. And you will wind up in a dark valley full of dry bones.* And you will wonder: ''How did I get in here?''

You got there because your dedication was not what it should have been. Your dedication to God, to your prayer language, and to your prayer life were lacking.

Remember: only people who pray get things from heaven. I love you, my brother or sister, and I am not writing this book just in order to play games with you. The Holy Ghost requires me to tell you the truth. If you don't pray much, you don't get very much from heaven. I can tell you that right now. If you have stopped praying in tongues, I urge you to get back into your prayer life again.

I speak in tongues probably ten to twenty times a day. To me, praying in tongues is like breathing. It just comes naturally. I want to pray in tongues every day. I want to keep my spirit in good shape. When I open my eyes in the morning, I want to tell Jesus that I love Him. I begin to worship and praise Him right there in my bed, and I continue praying in tongues when I go through my day.

You ask, ''Well, what do you do that for?''

Because the Devil and his demons are going to try to tempt me that day. Praying in tongues at the start of my day makes them leave me alone.

There is no telling what I might do in a meeting if the Holy Ghost tells me to do it. In one service I was holding, a little girl had been playing the viola. After I had been speaking about ten minutes, the Holy Ghost said to me, "Call that girl up here right now. Tell her that I said to play the viola, and I will heal the sick."

The girl started playing the viola, and I started speaking in tongues, just as the Lord told me to do. Sick people started coming to the front, and they were getting healed, all over the floor!

"You mean by themselves?"

No! Them and God! You can't get healed without God. I am telling you that the Lord is wonderful. He works in strange ways that the natural mind can't understand.

It's time that you start obeying the Lord and not neglect praying in tongues. Be a willing vessel. That way you will not only have victory in your own life, but God will use you.

Prayer

Let's obey what we've been taught now.

If you have a friend or a loved one that has a need, call their name before God. Say:

God, I bring _____ *before You right now. Father, I claim Your mighty power to bring victory to them in Jesus' name.*

Satan, take your hands off _____.
I claim victory for them in Jesus' name.

Now, pray in tongues for them.

If you have a personal need, say:

Heavenly Father, I come to You in Jesus' name. I claim Your power to give me complete victory. Victory is mine, in Jesus' name.

Now, pray in tongues for yourself!

Glory to God! Praise God! Give Him praise and thanks.

10

The Holy Spirit
Wants To Manifest
Through You!

You say, "I wish I could get myself in shape, Brother Norvel. Help me get myself in shape to receive the gifts of the Spirit, to do what God wants me to do."

You know how God got me in shape to receive the gifts of the Spirit easy? He began to burn. The fire of God began to burn the ways of men out of me and make me a vessel that His Spirit could manifest himself through, because I would allow Him to.

He wants to manifest Himself through you and me more, but you have to become a person that will allow Him to do it. You have to be like a piece of putty sometimes. Let God mold you and do what He wants to do with you.

I didn't know the fire of God would burn this stuff out of me.

I liked football. I liked other sports also, but I *liked* college football.

A number of years ago I was going to Augusta, Georgia. A friend of mine told me to look up some people when I got there. They were real precious people, a Church of God pastor and his wife.

They insisted that I stay at their house instead of checking into a motel. So I slept the night in the parsonage.

In the morning the pastor came up to me and said, "Norvel, I've been praying and the Lord told me that He wanted you to stay in my church and speak in my church on Sunday.''

I said, ''Pastor, I've already got my weekend planned. I'm going to leave here Saturday morning and I'm going to drive to the University of Georgia, and I'm going to watch Tennessee beat Georgia.''

''Well,'' he said, ''I'm just telling you what the Lord told me.''

''I'll come back and speak for you some other time, Pastor. I've got my weekend all planned,'' I said.

Oh, I wanted to see Tennessee beat Georgia, so bad!

''I'm just telling you what the Lord said,'' he said.

So I stayed another night. He came up to me on Friday night and said, ''Brother Norvel, the Lord moved upon me again, and He wanted me to tell you that He wanted you to stay here at the church and speak on Sunday.''

I said, ''Pastor, I already told you I'll come back some other time and speak in your church. I promise.''

He said, ''I'm just telling you what the Lord told me.''

The Lord hadn't told me not to go to the football game. *The reason he hadn't told me was because I hadn't asked him.* And I wasn't going to ask Him. I didn't have any intentions of asking Him. I had made up my mind what I was going to do this weekend. Then here comes this full gospel preacher trying to mess up my weekend.

I got to thinking about it a little bit, but I wasn't sold on it though. I wanted to see Tennessee beat Georgia so bad.

Saturday morning I got up and was going to leave before too long. The pastor came up to me and said, ''You haven't been to the church since you've been here. I want you to stop there and see our sanctuary on the way out. But,'' he said, ''you ought not to be leaving, Norvel. The Lord dealt with me again last night. He said He wants you to stay at my church and speak Sunday.''

"I've told you, Pastor," I said, "I want to see Tennessee beat Georgia."

"Just telling you what the Lord said," he said.

So I started out. I went out and opened up the trunk of my brand new wine-colored Cadillac and put my suitcase in. I went back to go in my bedroom to get my clothes bag. I got as far as the parsonage and the pastor's wife started talking to me.

I was just sitting there, minding my own business and all of a sudden my heart began to hurt. I started holding my chest.

She said, "Brother Hayes, do you want us to pray for you?"

I said, "No, uh, uh. Everything is okay. No, that's all right."

About that time, the phone rang. When she came back from answering it she said, "Our janitor just had a heart attack down at the church, a real severe heart attack." The pastor had called and asked us to pray for him. So we did.

She hit the floor and started praying. I hit the floor by the coffee table and started praying in the living room. She was praying and praying and I was praying and praying. While we were praying, the phone rang again.

When she got up and went to answer it, all of a sudden in me, the Holy Ghost just went *bloop* and joy began to boil out of me. I felt so good I couldn't hardly stand it. That pain I was having in my heart just left. I thought the Lord had healed him.

Then she came back in and said, "The janitor is dead."

I thought, uh, then what in the world was that? (But the Lord showed me that same type of manifestation again when a girl died. He showed me that she went to heaven.)

She said, "He wasn't even saved. His wife is saved, but he wasn't saved, Brother Norvel. We never could get him saved."

The man owned the store across the street from the church. He just wanted to do the janitorial work for the church to help them. But he wasn't saved.

She asked me, "Will you go over to the store with me and tell his wife?"

I said, "Oh, yeah, sure. Something like this happens, I don't have to leave now. Sure, I'll go."

We got in the car and went to the store. We called the lady out from behind the counter and told her to sit down.

The pastor's wife said, "I'm going to have to tell you something. Your husband just died."

The lady broke and started crying. We started praying for her.

About the time we finished praying, the assistant pastor walked in. I was standing there talking to him when suddenly, the Spirit of God came upon me and said, "Go over to the church and pray." I was standing there, just shaking, in the store.

"When the pastor comes back," I said, "Tell him I'll be over at the church praying. God told me to go to the church and pray."

What did God want me to go to the church and pray for?

He wanted me to go to the church and pray because I didn't have much sense. God always wants you to pray, especially for yourself, when you're still goofed up.

I walked in the side door of that church toward the pulpit. As I did, God's power moved on me and by the time I got there, He just melted me to the floor. And I mean, just melted me — laid me out on the floor.

I began to pray in tongues, supernaturally, the Holy Ghost through me. I prayed in tongues for I guess, maybe two hours, just about as hard and fast as I could, making intercession in tongues.

Then, *I got beyond tongues.* The Spirit of God began to groan through me. And the fire of God came. I could feel in my flesh, junk (including football games) being burned out of me. I felt the fire of God burning everything out of me.

I laid on the floor and the Spirit of God groaned through me, maybe two hours. After a couple more hours went by, He just stopped.

I pushed myself up to a sitting position. I couldn't get up off the floor. Everything seemed like it had been burned out of me. My flesh seemed like it had things just burned out of it. I had no desire to go to a football game. It was too late anyway. Tennessee had already beaten Georgia while I was on the floor, flat on my back, groaning before God. Fire came down from the Spirit world and burned football games out of me. (I think I've been to one more since then.)

God can burn golf courses out of you, if it keeps you away from the work of God. There is nothing wrong with playing a game of golf that I know of. But there is no use wasting a lot of time playing golf and going to football games, if you're not going to pass out any tracts.

The fire of God can come and burn it out of you.

Make up your mind that you'll do what God wants you to do. Say, "Jesus, help me to do what You want me to do. I love You Jesus. I want my life to count for You. I know, Jesus, that I've only got one chance to win souls, not two. Help me to be God's man, full of power, full of love, and full of holy boldness."

Brother, Sister, there is nothing wrong with you today but what the fire of God, the groaning of the Holy Ghost, will come and deliver you from it. I don't care what it is. Groaning before God will burn the chaff out of you.

> **Likewise the Spirit also helpeth our infirmities: for we know not what we should pray for as we ought: but the Spirit itself maketh intercession for us with groanings which cannot be uttered.**
>
> **And he that searcheth the hearts knoweth what is the mind of the Spirit, because he maketh intercession for the saints according to the will of God.**
>
> **Romans 8:26,27**

That is what He did, with tongues and groanings, making intercession for Norvel Hayes in Augusta, Georgia. For what? To get the will of God for me.

What was the will of God for me? To go and see Tennessee beat Georgia in football, or stay in the church and speak on Sunday?

The Holy Ghost got the will of God for me.

When I raised up and sat, leaning on one arm, the pastor and the assistant pastor were sitting there. I couldn't even get up. I said, "Okay, Pastor, I'll speak in your church Sunday."

He said, "I know it."

I said, "Yeah, I guess you do."

I spoke on Sunday morning, and I gave an invitation at about 12:30 p.m. When I gave the invitation, they started running to the altar and got all over the floor, everywhere. God's Spirit started moving on those people. Many people got blessed.

I started to go back to the pulpit and turn around to close the service. (I looked at a clock and it was 20 minutes until 2:00.)

A young couple (about 21 years old) came down the aisle. They had just gotten married. The young man said, "We've never been in a service like this before. Mr. Hayes, we've been watching this for two hours and I know this

176

is real. I've got sense enough to see that. My wife and me want to get saved.''

Just think, if I had closed the service at 1:30, they might have gone to hell. He wasn't impressed at 1:30. He didn't get up at 1:30. He got out of his seat at 20 minutes until 2:00. The Spirit of God was trying to sell him, but he wasn't completely sold at 1:30. (When a salesman comes and tries to sell you something, you're not sold until you start getting the money out of your pocket and pay him.) He wasn't sold until 20 minutes until 2:00. Does it pay to obey the Holy Spirit?

After church, they took me out to eat with a whole bunch of people from the church. As soon as I sat down I said, ''As soon as I get through eating, I'm going to go out to the parsonage, get my clothes and drive back to Cleveland, Tennessee. I'm going home.''

The pastor said, ''Oh no you're not. I'm going to get a revival out of this.''

I said, ''Pastor, no. No revival, Pastor. I'm not going to stay. I've got some things I have to do tomorrow morning. I'm going home.''

He said, ''Oh no you're not. I'm going to get a revival out of this.''

''I'm going home,'' I said.

You might ask, ''What did Jesus say about it?''

I don't know, I didn't ask Him. I wanted to do what I wanted to do.

Most of the time, when you come out of a service like that, you're kind of weak because you've prayed with people so long. Most of the time, when you begin to eat food, you'll start gaining a little strength.

This was the *only* time in my life, every bite of food I took, I got weaker. After I got through eating, they got me to the car. By the time they got me back to the parsonage, the pastor's wife turned the bed down. By the time they got me in bed, I was just like a rag that had been wrung out. I went off to sleep.

I woke up at 5:30 p.m. and I felt like a jack rabbit. It was too late to go home.

"It's too late to go home, Brother Norvel," the pastor said. "Jesus wants you to speak tonight."

I said, "I know it. Okay, Pastor. Okay."

The service started at 7:00 p.m. At 20 minutes until 11:00 p.m., a very well-dressed man with diamond rings on his fingers and diamond stick pins, came strolling down to the altar.

He said, "This is the first time I have sat some place for four hours and didn't smoke a cigarette. I've never seen anything like this. I'd like to find God myself, but I've been married before. The wife I am living with now and I have two children. I met some Christians (I own a jewelry store over in another city), and they said if I gave my life to Jesus, I'd have to get rid of my wife and children now, and go back and marry my first wife again. And I love the girl I'm married to now and I love my little children. I don't want to give them away. That's the reason I rejected Jesus. I don't want to give them away. Is that true, Mister?"

I said, "There is no use in trying to unscramble an egg. Forget it. Are you willing to drop on your knees right now and ask Jesus to forgive you of all your sins, and ask Him to come into your heart by faith? Are you willing to do that, Mister?"

"Yeah," he said. "I'm willing to do that."

"Show me," I said.

He looked at me, dropped on his knees and started crying out to God for mercy and help. Right there on his knees, he gave his life to God and got saved.

Just think, what if I had closed the service at 10:30 p.m.? Now there's two in one day.

Why? Because of the fire of God, speaking in tongues, groaning before God, burning the football games out of me, keeping me laid out on the floor so I could stay there. And maybe, because I didn't go to that *one* football game, there's a good chance of dozens and maybe even hundreds of people coming into the family of God.

You might say, "Well that's good, Norvel. That's good to love the Lord that much."

Listen to me Brother and Sister, I hate to tell you this: I loved Jesus then, and I love Jesus now; but I didn't love Jesus enough to not go to the football game. The Holy Ghost that lives inside of me made intercession for me with groanings which cannot be uttered. He delivered me. *The Holy Ghost made intercession for me.*

Right now I have the testimony of salvation of those two young people and that man who owned the jewelry store because from the Spirit world, down from heaven, come weapons to the Church: God's weapons.

I'd like to tell you that there is some easy sweet precious way of getting the junk out of you, but I'm sorry to have to tell you, Brother and Sister, you'll have to come the way of tongues. You'll have to come the way of groanings before God. The Holy Ghost needs to come through you, and set you free.

Get yourself ready to receive the gifts of the Spirit.

Books by Norvel Hayes

How To Live and Not Die

The Winds of God
Bring Revival

God's Power Through
the Laying on of Hands

The Blessing of Obedience

Stand in the Gap
for Your Children

How To Get
Your Prayers Answered

Endued With Power

Prostitute Faith

The Number One Way
To Fight the Devil

Why You Should
Speak in Tongues

What To Do for Healing

How To Triumph
Over Sickness

Financial Dominion —
How To Take Charge
of Your Finances

The Healing Handbook

Rescuing Souls
From Hell —
Handbook for
Effective Soulwinning

How To Cast Out Devils

Visions — The Window to the
Supernatural

Radical Christianity

Secrets To Keeping
Your Faith Strong

Putting Your Angels
To Work

Know Your Enemy

**Available from your local bookstore,
or by writing:**

Harrison House
P. O. Box 35035 • Tulsa, OK 74153

Norvel Hayes shares God's Word boldly and simply, with an enthusiasm that captures the heart of the hearer. He has learned through personal experience that God's Word can be effective in every area of life and that it will work for anyone who will believe it and apply it.

Norvel owns several businesses which function successfully despite the fact that he spends more than half his time away from the office, ministering the Gospel throughout the country. His obedience to God and his willingness to share his faith have taken him to a variety of places. He ministers in churches, seminars, conventions, colleges, prisons — anywhere the Spirit of God leads.

For a complete list of tapes and
books by Norvel Hayes, write:

Norvel Hayes
P. O. Box 1379
Cleveland, TN 37311

*Please include your prayer requests
and comments when you write.*

In Canada contact:

Word Alive
P. O. Box 284
Niverville, Manitoba
CANADA R0A 1E0

For international sales in Europe,
contact:

Harrison House Europe
Belruptstrasse 42 A
A — 6900 Bregenz
AUSTRIA

The Harrison House Vision

Proclaiming the truth and the power
Of the Gospel of Jesus Christ
With excellence;

Challenging Christians to
Live victoriously,
Grow spiritually,
Know God Intimately.